1,000,000 Books
are available to read at

www.ForgottenBooks.com

Read online
Download PDF
Purchase in print

ISBN 978-1-331-12321-7
PIBN 10147909

This book is a reproduction of an important historical work. Forgotten Books uses state-of-the-art technology to digitally reconstruct the work, preserving the original format whilst repairing imperfections present in the aged copy. In rare cases, an imperfection in the original, such as a blemish or missing page, may be replicated in our edition. We do, however, repair the vast majority of imperfections successfully; any imperfections that remain are intentionally left to preserve the state of such historical works.

Forgotten Books is a registered trademark of FB &c Ltd.
Copyright © 2018 FB &c Ltd.
FB &c Ltd, Dalton House, 60 Windsor Avenue, London, SW19 2RR.
Company number 08720141. Registered in England and Wales.

For support please visit www.forgottenbooks.com

1 MONTH OF FREE READING

at

www.ForgottenBooks.com

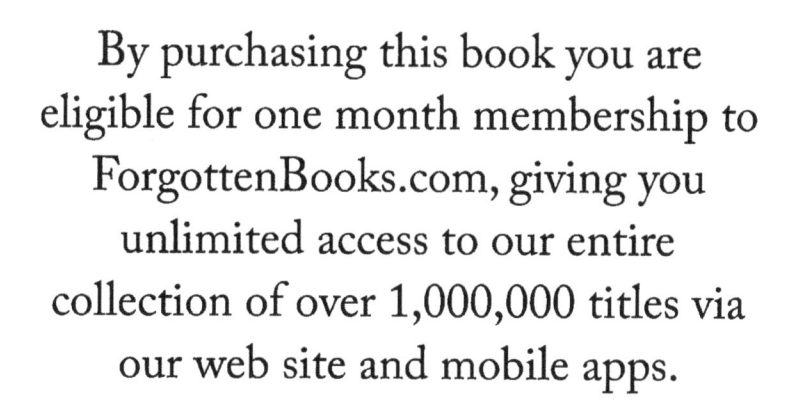

By purchasing this book you are eligible for one month membership to ForgottenBooks.com, giving you unlimited access to our entire collection of over 1,000,000 titles via our web site and mobile apps.

To claim your free month visit: www.forgottenbooks.com/free147909

* Offer is valid for 45 days from date of purchase. Terms and conditions apply.

English
Français
Deutsche
Italiano
Español
Português

www.forgottenbooks.com

Mythology Photography **Fiction**
Fishing Christianity **Art** Cooking
Essays Buddhism Freemasonry
Medicine **Biology** Music **Ancient Egypt** Evolution Carpentry Physics
Dance Geology **Mathematics** Fitness
Shakespeare **Folklore** Yoga Marketing
Confidence Immortality Biographies
Poetry **Psychology** Witchcraft
Electronics Chemistry History **Law**
Accounting **Philosophy** Anthropology
Alchemy Drama Quantum Mechanics
Atheism Sexual Health **Ancient History**
Entrepreneurship Languages Sport
Paleontology Needlework Islam
Metaphysics Investment Archaeology
Parenting Statistics Criminology
Motivational

BEOWULF

PRESS NOTICES OF PREVIOUS EDITION.

The *Athenæum* says—

"Colonel Lumsden has certainly succeeded in producing a readable and most agreeable version of this interesting monument of our language."

The *Academy* says—

"A vigorous and readable English version, in good swinging ballad metre."

The *St. James' Gazette* says—

"The vigour of the original has been very faithfully reproduced; notably so in the account of the hero's fight with Grendel's mother, in the depths of the haunted mere."

The *Reliquary* says—

"We cordially commend the book, and assure our readers that in adding it to their literary stores they are indeed acquiring that which will give them pleasure, and be of permanent value."

LONDON: KEGAN PAUL, TRENCH & CO.

                    ...ne he þy ær...
oðer þone ongean daguþ sy...
fold buende no hie fæder cunnon
him ænig wæs ær acenned dyrnra ga...
hie dygel lond warigeað wulf hleoþu
nessas frecne fengelad ðær fyrgen
stream under næssa genipu niþer ge...
flod under foldan nis þæt heoru...
mearc þes mere stande ð ofer þæm ho...
gim hrinde bearwas wudu wyrtum fæst
wæter oferhelmað þær mæg nihta ge...
niðwundor seon fyr on flode no þæs frod...
leofað gumena bearna þone grund wit...
ðeah þe hæð stapa hundum geswenced hea...
hior nu hunu hole wudu sece feor...
flymed ær he feorh seleð aldor on ofre ær...
he in wille hafelan (ne is) þ heoru seop þonon
yð ge blond up astigeð won to wolcnum þon
wind styreþ lað ge þewer oð þ lyft drysmaþ
rodoras reotað nu is se ræd ge lang eft æt...

BEOWULF

AN OLD ENGLISH POEM

TRANSLATED INTO MODERN RHYMES

BY

LIEUT.-COLONEL H. W. LUMSDEN
LATE ROYAL ARTILLERY

SECOND EDITION, REVISED AND CORRECTED

LONDON
KEGAN PAUL, TRENCH & CO., 1, PATERNOSTER SQUARE
1883

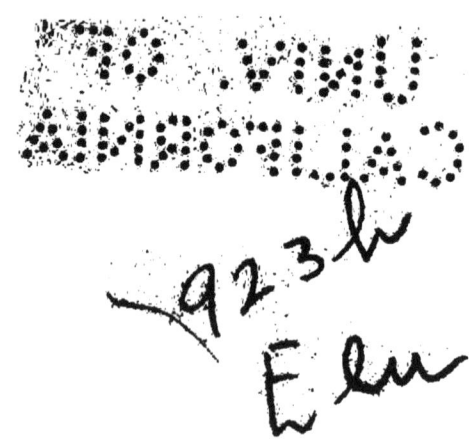

923h
E lu

24496

(All rights of translation and of reproduction are reserved.)

PREFACE TO THE SECOND EDITION.

In this edition I have endeavoured to remove some of the blunders which disfigured its predecessor, but many, I fear, have escaped my notice. Some parts have been entirely rewritten, and the passages formerly omitted as obscure or uninteresting have been inserted. Such as it is, the translation is now complete. A few notes have been added; and the introduction has been materially altered and, I hope, improved.

The Anglo-Saxon diphthong *ea* is so liable to mispronunciation when reproduced in modern English, that I have thought it better to strike out the *e* in such names as Healfdene, etc. Halfdene is at any rate nearer the true form than H*ea*lfdene, as he ran some risk of being called.

The lines of the original poem are given at the top of each page.

An autotype of a page of the manuscript (on a reduced scale) faces the title-page of this volume. It contains lines 1354–1377 (see p. 65), and reads thus in Heyne's edition of 1873:—

> næfne he wæs mára þonne ænig man óðer
> þone on geár-dagum Grendel nemdon
> foldbúende : no hie fæder cunnon
> hwæðer him ænig wæs ær ácenned
> dyrnra gásta. Hie dýgel land
> warigeað, wulthleoðu, windige næssas,
> frécne fengelád, þær fyrgenstreám
> under næssa genipu niðer gewiteð,
> flód under foldan. Nis þæt feor heonan
> mílgemearces þæt se mere standeð,
> ofer þæm hongiað hrinde bearwas
> wudu wyrtum fæst wæter oferhelmað.
> Þær mæg nihta gehwæm niðwundor seón
> fýr on flóde ; nó þæs fród leofað
> gumena bearna þæt þone grund wite:
> þeáh þe heað-stapa bundum geswenced
> heorot hornum trum holtwudu séce
> feorran geflýmed, ær he feorh seleð,
> aldor on ófre, ær he in wille
> hafelan [hýdan]. Nis þæt beórn stóv :
> þonon ýðgeblond up ástígeð
> won to wolcnum, þonne wind styreð
> láð gewidru óð þæt lyft drysmað
> roderas reótað. Nú is ræd gelang
> eft æt

INTRODUCTION.

IN the beginning of the last century Humphrey Wanley, who was employed by the great Anglo-Saxon scholar Hickes to make a catalogue of all the Anglo-Saxon MSS. to be found in the kingdom, discovered in the library of Sir Robert Cotton a volume containing, with other things, a 'tractatus nobilissimus poetice scriptus'—the poem of Beowulf. This is the only MS. of the poem in existence, and it is now with the rest of the Cottonian MSS. in the British Museum. It is a parchment codex, written probably in the tenth century, the transcript of a work composed at a much earlier date. It was injured by a fire which in 1731 consumed a part of the Cottonian Library, but the damage done, though irretrievable, happily does not go far. After this mishap it slumbered undisturbed until

1786, when Thorkelin, a Danish scholar who had been attracted by Wanley's account of the MS., had it transcribed, and laboured on it for twenty years. He was just about to publish it when the British fleet bombarded Copenhagen, his house caught fire, and most of his papers were burnt. But his transcript escaped, and nothing daunted he set to work again, and in 1815 he published the poem for the first time. The interest thus awakened has gone on increasing. In England Thorpe, Kemble, and quite recently Mr. Arnold, have put forth editions of the work; and in Germany many scholars have laboured on it, of whom I need here only mention the chief, Grein and Heyne. The Early English Text Society has this year published an autotype of the entire MS.

Beowulf is the oldest heroic poem in any dialect of the great Gothic family—earlier probably by some centuries than the heroic poems of the Edda—earlier by an even longer period than the Heldenbuch and the Nibelungenlied; and it stands alone, beyond all question or comparison the most interesting and the most original of all the literary works bequeathed to us by our forefathers.

Although much of it is at best only legendary, and a great deal purely fabulous, there can be no doubt, I think, that we have, imbedded in the wild fancies of the story, a dim and vague but authentic record of the doings of our aucestors some fourteen centuries ago. Dr. Grein, indeed, ranks it higher as an historical authority than the later Sagas which deal with the same period, or 'the confused statements of the learned Saxo-Grammaticus;' * but this after all is no very great praise; and if the poem were only a document by means of which we could make a little clearer the obscure and uninteresting history of Danes and Geáts in the fifth century it would not be worth much. Its real value—considered as an historical authority merely—lies in the vivid picture it gives us of the life, the manners, and the habits of thought and speech of our forefathers in that "dark backward and abysm of time." We have it here at first hand, 'proving,' in Chapman's words,

"—how firm truth builds in poet's feigning;"

and it is scarcely an exaggeration to say that we may live with our ancestors and know them—

* See his article in the Jahrbuch f. Engl. u. Roman Literatur, vol. iv.

which surely is the chief end of history—better in this poem than in all the bulky volumes of professed historians.

That some of the persons mentioned in the poem are historical there can be little doubt, but of the hero himself the utmost we can assert is, that he may not impossibly have been a real man. The two theories about him propounded by Kemble show in a very striking manner the difficulty of the question. In 1833 the great Anglo-Saxon scholar has no doubt that Beowulf is historical; in 1837 he retracts the erroneous views developed in the earlier volume, and Beowulf becomes a mere phantom of mythology. The truth probably lies somewhere between these extreme views, and indeed Kemble would very likely have modified his later theory if he had known of the identification of Higelac, the uncle of Beowulf, with the 'Chochilaicus, the King of the Danes,' whose death in battle with the *Attoarii* in 511 is recorded by Gregory of Tours, and in the *Gesta Regum Francorum*. The dry record of these chroniclers is a remarkable confirmation of the passages in the poem which tell of Higelac's fatal expedition to Friesland and slaughter by the Hetwars, and we thus get, what Kemble craved in vain, a key-date of the highest value.* A farther trace of Higelac is found in the passage from a writer of the tenth century, quoted by Grein in the article already referred to, which relates that the bones of *Huiglaicus qui imperavit Getis et a Francis occisus est* were still preserved on an island in the Rhine, near its mouth, and shown to strangers as a wonder for their immense size.

If then it is pretty certain that the uncle really lived, why should we doubt the existence of the nephew merely because a heap of fables has gathered round his name? We have no record of him, it is true, elsewhere. In the shadowy realm of Northern history or legend he is unknown, but not assuredly, as the poem testifies, *caret quia vate sacro.* Anglo-Saxon and Norse genealogies are alike silent about him; but this may be explained by the fact that

---

* The Hetwars are evidently the *Attoarii*. They are identified with the *Catti* of Tacitus, as their neighbours the Hugas are with his *Chauci*. The fact that Chochilaicus is called King of the 'Danes' is of no moment. The ecclesiastical historian probably used the word as including northern barbarians of all kinds. If Tacitus's glowing description of the Catti remained true it is little wonder that the Hetwars overcame the Goths. *Alios ad prælium ire videas, Cattos ad bellum* (Ger. 30).

he was a childless man, and after his death his little kingdom was probably soon swallowed up in the dominions of greater neighbours. On the whole, therefore, if we have little reason to affirm his existence we have as little to deny it, and though we may not place him on the *terra firma* of reality, we may yet justly refuse to consign him absolutely to the cloudland of mythology.

In that hazy region—

"Where nothing is, but all things seem,"

his name is analyzed, and is found to mean 'cultivator,' with an honorary termination, 'wulf.' He is the god of husbandry; he is Thor struggling with the great serpent; he is, in short, whatever anybody may choose to read *into* his name and story. It would not be difficult, I think, to extract a myth of the dawn fighting with the powers of darkness from the tale of Beowulf going with his twelve companions to do battle with the dragon; and something might even be made out of Grendel, who is expressly called 'the servant of evening,' and his more terrible mother, by any one with a taste for inquiries of this kind. In all such theories there is no doubt a kernel of truth. The sources of the Grendel and the dragon stories must be sought in the vast Serbonian bog of Gothic legend—nay, even farther afield—and the most resolute stickler for the historical reality of the hero himself will hardly deny the mythical nature of his adventures.

But I utterly reject all rationalizing interpretations of his marvellous exploits. Grendel and his mother, we are told, mean hurricanes and inundations, but Beowulf purifies "seas and all wide land," and thus cultivation, and so forth, triumphs over the forces of nature. Or—and this time it is even Grein who suggests it—Grendel means the attacks of pirates from which Beowulf delivered the Danes. At this rate Grendel may mean anything. One might hazard a theory that he was bad drainage, fatal to the sleepers in the hall that Hrothgar had built at Heorot, until Beowulf, with improved sanitary arrangements, came to the rescue of the distressed householder and put things right. The fiery dragon, again, might be only an imperfect water supply, which Beowulf—not unlike Faust in his old age—cured with dams and canals and reservoirs, and so got untold wealth. But why should we always try to explain away whatever seems strange to us? *We* do not believe in fiends and fiery dragons, but the poet of Beowulf did, and I think he would have opened the eyes of astonishment if he had been told that he only meant night and darkness, hurricanes, inundations, and the attack of pirates.

Whether Beowulf really lived or not, the poem asserts that he was a Geát. Who were the Geáts? Kemble maintained that they were Angles; but eminent scholars have found serious objections to this theory, and all the best authorities, I believe, now agree in identifying them with the Goths of the Swedish province of Gotland. The prefix 'Weder' is supposed to indicate the inhabitants of the 'weather' or western side of the peninsula. Unhappily the name of Higelac's capital is nowhere given.* The modern Gottenborg, however, both in name and position answers very well to the description of the "burg," in which the Gothic king dwelt, and whence Beowulf set sail on his voyage to Heorot. Gustavus Adolphus, when he founded the city, may have availed himself of an old site and an old name.

* Kemble, I hardly know why, calls Hrafnesholt, "the Raven's wood" (Part III. vi.), Higelac's capital, and identifies it with Ravensburg in Sleswick.—(Beowulf, vol. i., Preface, p. xvii.)

INTRODUCTION.

Moreover, on an island a little higher up the river on which Gottenborg stands, at a point where the stream divides into two channels to reach the sea, are the ruins of a stronghold built by the Norwegian king Hakon IV. in 1308. The name of this place is Bôhûs, which, according to Grein, means *domus Boi*, and as *Bous* is identical with the *Beaw*, or *Beow*, of the genealogies, we may have here some trace of the Beowulf of the poem. "Beowulf's mound," says Grein, must be sought on some promontory in the neighbourhood, and it may be, he adds, that close inquiry might still find some tradition of the hero lingering among the country folk.

But what connection have Swedish Goths with England? and why should an English poet celebrate with such enthusiasm the great exploits in Denmark and in Gotland of a Gothic hero? Thorpe's reply to such questions is that the poem is founded on a lost Norse Saga brought to England, and translated during the sway of the Danish dynasty in the eleventh century.* But to this Mr. Arnold's rejoinder is crushing and conclusive. Such a poem, he says, "could not in England above all countries—

* Thorpe's Beowulf, Preface, p. viii.

b

'While yet her cicatrice looked raw and red
Under the Danish sword'—

have called forth any feelings but those of aversion and disgust."

Mr. Arnold's own theory is exceedingly ingenious. After calling attention to the missionary activity which prevailed in Wessex towards the end of the seventh century, and which sent many men abroad to preach the Gospel among the Frisians, Germans, and Danes, he tells us the story of St. Willibrord, who landed in Friesland in 690, and visited Denmark in 695. The king of the Danes allowed him to take thirty young men back with him into Friesland to be educated in the Christian faith. Now what difficulty is there, Mr. Arnold asks, "in supposing that these young Danes, or some of them, were steeped in the mythology and hero-worship which at that time reigned in the North? . . . What difficulty in supposing that the half mythical, half historical traditions of their own and the neighbouring countries were known to them? . . . The materials out of which the poem of *Beowulf* is composed (a portion of them being probably the old Folks-lieder and Sagas themselves retained in the memory) might in this way have all been naturally conveyed to some Anglo-Saxon priest, a companion or friend of Willibrord, who loved the poetry and language of his own race, and saw how, by selection among these materials, a great and harmonious poem might be constructed. ... It is more probable that the author was a churchman than a layman; but if so, he was a churchman *in a lay mood.*"* Ingenious as this is, it seems to me only to add to our difficulties. The nineteenth century is not unacquainted with lay-minded churchmen, but no amount of "intellectual activity in Wessex" can reconcile me to such a phenomenon as an ecclesiastic, and above all a missionary, of that type in the year 700. The poems of Andreas and Elene, to which Mr. Arnold refers as analogous cases, seem to me absolutely different. The legendary adventures of a saint, and the story of the invention of the cross, are precisely the subjects on which a churchman's imagination would delight to dwell, and which he would weave, or cause to be woven, into "lively and stirring poems." For them the learning which

* Arnold's Beowulf, Introduction, pp. xxx.-xxxiii. This theory is suggested too by Mr. Green, 'Making of England,' p. 162.

was the exclusive possession of the clergy was indispensable; but for Beowulf the priest is a needless excrescence. It is the layman here, not the ecclesiastic, who is the depositary of the requisite knowledge; and there seems no necessity for clerical intervention at any stage of the process which transformed an unwritten mass of tradition into an elaborate poem.

Without presuming to enter into a discussion for which I am, as Falstaff says, "heinously unprovided," I may remark that the 'Danes' had been from of old time, and in other regions as well as here, the neighbours and close allies of the Geáts, if they were not actually of the same blood.* Besides 'Danes' simply, the subjects of Hrothgar are called in the poem Gar-, Bright-, Ring-, East-, West-, South-, and North-Danes. The first three of these prefixes are probably mere honorific titles; but the other four seem to imply that 'Danes' of all points of the compass were members of one family, of one blood, and (though possibly with dialectic differences) of one speech; and that the 'King of Danes' ruled over them all, either with a real kingly sway or with the more

* Grimm, Gesch. der Deutschen Sprache, 190–193.

shadowy power of overlord. His dominion appears to have extended over Jutland (which in the early centuries of our era was certainly occupied by a Germanic race), for Hengest, the leader of the Jutes, served under Halfdene, and one of Hrothgar's nobles was 'chief of the Wendels,' *i.e.* Wendill in Jutland. Grimm places East-Danes in Schonen, West-Danes in the islands, and North-Danes he pronounces to be Jutes.*

But in the poem the Danes, collectively, are also called by two names, which are of great significance and importance—'Ingwines' and 'Hréðmen.' The former have been clearly identified with the Ingævones;† the latter

* D.S. 735. "The Danes of Beda," says Mr. Hyde Clarke, "so far from being Scandinavians, were Suevians. Jutland and its neighbourhood were in the Roman time Suevian, but when the English, Saxons, Frisians, and Warings swarmed forth by land and sea, the land, which Beda says was waste and empty, was filled up again by Slavs from the east and Scandinavians from the north. ... Thus it was that the earlier or Suevian Danes came into Britain" (Transactions of the Royal Historical Society, 1878).

† Zeuss, however, seems to think that 'Ingwine's lord' is a name of honour connected with Yngvi, a name of the god Freyr (Die Deutschen und die Nachbarstämme, p. 74).

Grimm * identifies with the Reudigni of Tacitus, and both of these were without question Germanic, not Scandinavian, peoples.

It would appear, then, that at the period of which the poem treats, the countries forming the modern kingdom of Denmark were occupied by various kindred tribes—some of them undoubtedly Germanic, and all, collectively, known by Germanic names, as well as by that of 'Danes.' From the internal evidence supplied by the poem, therefore, may it not be inferred that these 'Danes' were the brethren in blood and speech of Angles, Frisians, and Saxons, and that they, as well as their neighbours the Goths, shared, possibly under the name of Jutes, in the conquest of Britain? In that case it would be only natural, that the traditions and legends, which were the common property of Danes and Goths, and which clustered round the name of a real or mythical hero and deliverer, should have been brought to England in popular songs and ballads, and should in due time have been fused together into the poem of Beowulf.

If there is any truth, then, in this theory, the

* D. S. 741.

poem tells us not of foreign races, but of our own ancestors, of the romantic achievements of a hero of our own blood, and of the wars and feuds which raged as hotly on the continent of Europe between the various tribes from which we spring, as in after days between Wessex, Mercia, and Northumbria, or between England and Scotland.

At the time it was composed the poet's work may have been very popular: we can certainly point to passages in which his turn of phrase has been imitated by later poets. But, meanwhile, words began to change their meaning. 'Danes' were no longer the ancestors of the singer and his hearers, but a new race of cruel and devastating foes; and so gradually a poem which opened with the name, and *seemed* to celebrate the glories of these ruthless enemies, fell into disrepute and neglect until there remained but one copy of it in existence preserved for us by a happy chance.

To determine the age of the poem we have two fixed dates. There is first the death of Higelac in 511, and the statement that Beowulf reigned for fifty winters after he succeeded to the throne. It cannot, therefore, be *earlier* than the end of the sixth century. Again, the mention of the Merovingians in the Messenger's speech in Part III. shows that that race still held nominal sway over the Franks when the poet wrote. It cannot, therefore, be *later* than 752. We are thus restricted to a period of about a century and a half within which the poem must have been written; and, if we grant that the hero really lived, this period is farther narrowed by the necessity of allowing a certain time to elapse after his death, to admit of his exploits assuming in popular belief the romantic guise in which they have come down to us. Hence, therefore, as well as from a comparison of the language of the poem with that of other works of known date, it is now, I believe, generally agreed that Beowulf, in its present form, belongs to the end of the seventh, or, according to Grein, 'at latest' the beginning of the eighth century.

The scene of the poem is laid in Denmark and in the land of the Geáts, wherever that may have been. Heorot is in Zealand, either at Hiortholm, as Grein thinks, or at Roskilde ('Ro's well'), which is said to have been built by Hroar the son of Haldan, as Hrothgar and

Healfdene are called in Norse tradition. To this there is, as far as I know, only one dissentient voice. Dr. Haigh * maintains, sometimes with plausibility, that the scene of the drama, and the actors in it, as well as the author, are all to be found in Anglia and Northumbria; but though the ingenuity of the learned writer never fails, and his theory is exceedingly seductive—one would so gladly hail Beowulf as a *national* epic in the fullest sense of the word—it seems to me that in escaping from all difficulties about the authorship of the poem, he encounters obstacles of another kind, especially in regard to the Traveller's Song, far more serious and more insurmountable; and, on the whole, one would rather bear the ills one has than fly to Dr. Haigh's.

Some writers have professed to find a 'genuine Pagan ring' in the poem. To me, I confess, it seems that the 'ring' is quite as much Christian. I willingly admit, indeed, that the Christianity is singularly colourless; the name of Christ is not once mentioned; nor is there the slightest allusion to any article of Christian faith. But

* 'The Anglo-Saxon Sagas,' by D. H. Haigh. London, 1861.

for all that, the pious little sermons, moral reflections, and religious phrases which occur in almost every page, are unmistakably Christian in spirit, and although some are manifest interpolations, many of them, as Mr. Sweet remarks, "are so incorporated into the poem that it is impossible to remove them without violent alterations of the text."* How, indeed, could it be otherwise? If the poet lived in England in the end of the seventh century he was of course a Christian; and the wonder seems to me to be, not that in recasting a mass of heathen legend he should have allowed his Christianity to be seen, but that he should have been so reticent. His religious faith plays like sunlight everywhere without disturbing the local colour, for although he was certainly a Christian, he as certainly had a deep sympathy with the heathen past. He stands alone in Old English literature as the representative of a class—not uncommon in a later age among the Icelanders, but unknown, I think, among every other people on

* 'Sketch of the history of Anglo-Saxon poetry' in Hazlitt's edition of Warton's 'History of English Poetry,' vol. ii. p. 10. Mr. Sweet agrees with Green in insisting on the 'remarkable unity and homogeneousness of the whole work.' Ib. p. 11.

the face of the earth—men who, Christians themselves, and removed only a very few generations from idolatry, yet looked back with pride on their heathen forefathers, and for kinship's sake dealt tenderly with their erring-faith. Of this class Snorri Sturluson is the best example, who, in spite of his indisputable orthodoxy, could yet, in the prose Edda, tell with sympathetic humour the stories of the old gods, and, in the Sagas of Olaf Tryggvason and St. Olaf, touch with strange gentleness the heathenism which those monarchs so unsparingly and even cruelly rooted out.

I ought, perhaps, to say a few words about the translation. It is as literal as I could make it, subject to the exigencies of metre and rhyme. Sometimes to clear up an ambiguous 'he' or 'him,' or to avoid the tiresome repetition, so common in Anglo-Saxon poetry, of a stereotyped form of words, in speaking of persons especially, I have substituted the proper name; but in spite of all my efforts, and I am very conscious of my shortcomings in this, as in other things, I cannot venture to hope that I have always, or often, succeeded in giving the sense of a difficult passage, or in making intelligible in the translation what in the original is dark and confused.

There are many words and phrases which must necessarily seem strange at first to readers unacquainted with the old language—'ringed-stem,' 'mead-bench,' 'ring-giver,' and the like; but their meaning is clear enough, and a full explanation of the ideas, manners, and customs which underlie these and similar phrases can easily be got elsewhere by those who wish it.

The alliterated rhythmical lines of Anglo-Saxon poetry are, perhaps, more artificial than any modern form of English verse, and an attempt to reproduce them, unless done with the consummate skill which Mr. Tennyson has shown in his translation of the Song of Brunanburh, would soon leave the ear at once wearied and unsatisfied. The common ballad measure has seemed to me on the whole the best fitted to give a close, but I hope a fairly readable, version of a work too little known to English readers. Although the original poem is divided into what may be called cantos, the divisions seem quite arbitrary, and are sometimes altogether inexplicable. I have, therefore, disregarded them, and have divided the translation so that each part shall contain, as nearly as possible, a separate adventure or stage in the development of the poem. The division into three parts, however, and their names, I owe to Mr. Arnold.

CONTENTS.

PART I.

GRENDEL.

		PAGE
I. The Scylding Kings	... ...	3
II. Hrothgar and Grendel		6
III. The Coming of Beowulf	...	11
IV. Hunferd and Beowulf ...		24
V. The Fight with Grendel	...	32
VI. The Pursuit of Grendel		39
VII. The Rejoicings at Heorot ...		43

PART II.

GRENDEL'S MOTHER.

I. The Woman of the Mere	... ...	61
II. The Return from the Battle	...	77
III. The Parting of Beowulf and Hrothgar		84
IV. The Return of Beowulf to his own Land	...	88

PART III.

THE FIRE DRAKE.

		PAGE
I.	How the Dragon got the Hoard and wasted the Land	105
II.	Beowulf's Speech	114
III.	The Fight with the Dragon	118
IV.	The Death of Beowulf	126
V.	Wiglaf and the Dastards	131
VI.	The Message Home	134
VII.	The Burning of Beowulf's Body	140

Notes   147

PART I.
GRENDEL.

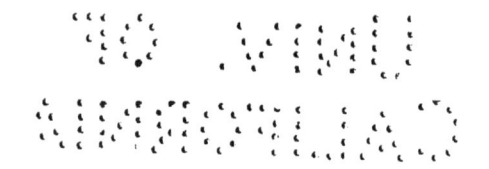

THE ARGUMENT.

Hrothgar the Scylding, the son of Halfdene, King of the Danes, builds a great mead-hall and calls it Heorot. There he dwells at peace dealing gifts to his people, and every day at the feast is joyous noise of song. But the fiend Grendel, vexed at the happiness of the Danes, comes down from the misty moors, and nightly kills and devours the sleepers in the hall. Twelve years this trouble lasts, and Hrothgar and his thanes are helpless and full of grief.

Beowulf the Scylfing, the son of Ecgtheow, and nephew of Higelac King of the Weder-Goths, makes ready a ship and sails to carry aid to Hrothgar in his need. The King bids him welcome, and gladly gives him leave to do battle with Grendel. At the feast Hunferd taunts Beowulf with having been beaten in a swimming match, and Beowulf tells the true story. Hrothgar and the Queen Waltheow are well pleased, and after the banquet the King gives the hall in charge to Beowulf and his comrades.

Grendel comes, and kills one of the men, but is seized by Beowulf, and hardly escapes, wounded to death, and leaving his arm behind him in Beowulf's grasp.

There is great joy in Heorot, and at night Hrothgar's thanes sleep in the hall as they did long ago.

BEOWULF.

I.

THE SCYLDING KINGS.

Lo! we have heard of glory won by Gar-Dane Kings of old,
And mighty deeds these princes wrought. Oft with his warriors bold,
Since first an outcast he was found, did Scyld the Scefing hurl
From their mead-benches many a folk, and frighted many an earl.
Therein he took his pleasure,—great he waxed beneath the sky,
And throve in worship, till to him all folk who dwelt hard by,
And o'er the whale-path, tribute paid, and did his word obey.
Good king was he!
    To him was born an heir in after day,

A child in hall; the gift of God to glad the people sent;
The deadly wrongs and woes He knew they long while underwent;
And therefore did the Prince of life, the Lord of glory, shower
All worldly praise on him, the famed Beowulf; and the power
Of Scyld's great heir spread far and wide through all the Danish land.
So must the young man gift and fee deal forth with open hand
To all his father's friends; thereby, in age and time of fight,
That comrades true may stand by him and help the folk aright.*
In every people men shall thrive by worthy deeds alone!
Then to God's hands went mighty Scyld, his fated hour made known,
And to the shore his comrades dear him carried as he bade
While yet as Scylding's chief beloved he long the people swayed.
   Ready at hithe the ringed-stem lay,—meet for a prince's bier—
Like ice it shone—and to her lap they bore their chieftain dear;

* Magna ... æmulatio ... principum cui plurimi et acerrimi comites. (Tacitus, Ger. 13.)

Hard by the mast they laid him down, their glorious
    lord of rings.
Well laden was the bark with wealth and far-brought
    precious things;
In comelier wise no keel I trow before did ever sail,
With weapons decked, and battle-weed, and bills,
    and coats of mail.
Much treasure lay upon his breast, with him afar to go
Into the might of waves. No lesser gifts did they
    bestow—
A people's gifts—than they who sent him forth in
    days of old
O'er seas, a little child, alone. A banner too of gold,
High o'er his head they raised aloft; and gave him
    to the flood
To bear away to open sea, with grief and mourning
    mood.
But not the wisest man in hall, nor bravest under
    heaven
Can ever tell for sooth to whom that lordly freight
    was driven.*
Then, when his father passed from earth Beowulf
    long while reigned,
The Scylding people's king beloved, and fame 'mong
    nations gained;
Till after him high Halfdene rose,—the fiery warrior
    old
Ruled the glad Scyldings all his life. To him in
    order told

        * See Note A.

Were born four children—Heregar, Hrothgar, and
    Halga good,
Leaders of hosts—and Elan who, so say the folk, was
    wooed
As queen by Ongentheow and shared the warrior
    Scylfing's bed.*
  To Hrothgar fame in war was given, and well in
    fight he sped,
So that his kinsmen willingly to him obedience gave,
And all the youths grew up to be a band of fighters
    brave.

II.

HROTHGAR AND GRENDEL.

To Hrothgar's mind it came to bid a lordly hall be
    framed,
A mead-house greater than had e'er 'mong sons of
    men been famed,
Wherein to deal to young and old the things that God
    had sent,
Save freeman's land and lives of men; and far the
    mandate went
To many a tribe on middle-earth to make the folk-
    stead fair.
So speedily it came to pass that high hall stateliest
    there

* See Note B.

Well ordered stood; and he whose word was mighty far and wide
Gave it the name of Heort. Nor was his promise true belied
When rings and wealth he dealt at feasts. With many a hornèd spire
High rose the hall—the raging glow to bide of dreadful fire!
  But no long time had passed away since under Hrothgar's yoke
His foes were brought, and bound by oaths to own his sway, when woke
The deadly sprite, who haunts the gloom; he could not brook to hear
Each day the joyous noise in hall, the minstrels' singing clear,
And melody of harp. For one, who knew of mankind's birth
In far-off times, thus sang: "The Lord Almighty made the earth,
Fair fields with water compassed round; and, glorious, set the light
Of sun and moon o'er every land to glad the people's sight;
And all the corners of the earth he decked with leaf and tree;
And every kind of life he made in all that living be!"
  For thus did all men happily and in great joyance dwell,
Till he began to work the foe—the evil fiend of hell!

That wicked sprite was Grendel hight; he trod the
　　outskirt waste,
And all amid the moors and fens he had his fastness
　　placed;
In the sea-monster's home long while, of bliss bereft,
　　he dwelt
Accursed of God. Upon Cain's race the Lord
　　eternal dealt
Vengeance for murdered Abel's blood; no peace got
　　Cain thereby,
Driven by the Lord for that foul sin far from mankind
　　to fly:
And from him sprang all monstrous things, eotens
　　sea-beasts and elves,
And giants whose long strife with God brought woe
　　upon themselves.
At nightfall Grendel took his way to spy the lofty
　　house,
To see how there the Ring-Danes dwelt after the
　　beer-carouse.
Their feasting o'er, a troop of knights, heedless of
　　coming woe,
He found asleep; and, grim and greedy, soon did
　　man's dark foe,
Fierce, terrible, in slumber deep snatch thirty thanes
　　away;
And homeward with rich spoil he turned, rejoicing in
　　his prey.
　　But in the twilight hour of dawn was Grendel's
　　　　ravage known

And loud uprose the morning cry, and feasting turned to moan.
  Grief-stricken sat the mighty lord, for thanes his sorrow swelled
When of that hateful sprite accursed the footprints he beheld;
Trouble too heavy weighed on him, loathly and lasting long;
And ere much time was past the fiend, shunning nor feud nor wrong,
But fast against them set, one night a yet worse murder wrought.
Then easily might he be found who quiet slumber sought,
And got himself a bed elsewhere in bower far away,
When Grendel's hate by tokens clear thus plain and open lay!
He who escaped the fiend thenceforth himself kept safe afar.
And thus alone against them all did Grendel wrongful war,
Till idle stood the stately house.
                              So mickle time went by;
Twelve winters did the Scyldings' lord in woe and trouble lie,
And boundless grief.
            And so to men 'twas told in mournful song
And clearly known how Grendel strove and waged with Hrothgar long

A war of hate and crime and feud,—long years of
 endless strife.
Peace would he none, nor stay the plague, nor take a
 price for life
For any man of Danish kin. Nor at the murderer's
 hand
Could any of the Witan hope in happier case to stand.
Like death's dark shadow thus the fiend harassed old
 knights and young,
Waylaid and plotted; and all night round misty
 moorlands hung.
(Men know not whither fiends of hell will sometimes
 take their way.)
Thus many crimes the foe of man alone that walketh
 aye,
Did often work and grievous wrong. All Heorot was
 his own—
The rich-dyed hall—in darksome night; yet to the
 kingly throne,
Dear in God's sight, he might not come, His love he
 might not know.
 Thus on the Scyldings' ruler lay heart-break and
 bitter woe;
In secret oft the nobles sat, and counsel sought to
 rede
What valiant men might fittest do in this dread time of
 need;
And sometimes at their idol shrines they sacrifices made,
And their false god with many words besought to give
 them aid

Against the people's woes.   Their custom this, the heathen's faith,
Whose thoughts were turned on hell.   The Lord they knew not—He who saith
Judgment of deeds ; of God they wist not ; nor to them was given
To worship glory's Lord aright—the Ruler of the heaven.
Woe unto him who thrusts his soul down to the arms of fire
By wicked hate !   No change in aught, no joy let him desire !
But well for him who seeks the Lord after his dying day
And in the Father's bosom finds a quiet rest alway !

III.

THE COMING OF BEOWULF.

Thus on his sorrow Halfdene's son was brooding evermore,
Nor could his grief the hero wise assuage ; for all too sore,
Loathly and lasting long, the straits that did the folk assail,
The tribulation all too fierce—the worst of nightly bale.
  Of Grendel's deeds the tidings reached a valiant Gothic knight,
Highborn, a thane of Higelac ; no mortal man in might

In this life's day was like to him. A goodly ship he
    bade
Make ready the swan's path to sail, that he might
    carry aid
To that great lord, the warrior king, now in his time
    of need.
And, though they loved him well, wise churls but
    lightly blamed the deed,
They looked for happy end to come, and whetted his
    bold mind.
  Now had he chosen fighting men, the keenest he
    could find
Of Gothic race; fifteen in all down to the ship they
    went.
A seaman skilled the landmarks told; and now the
    time was spent;
Below the cliff the vessel lay afloat upon the tide,
And while the waves broke on the sand the heroes
    climbed her side.
Into her lap a gleaming freight of goodly arms they
    bore,
And then they pushed with willing hearts the close-
    ribbed bark from shore.
  Now foamy-throated o'er the seas the ship before
    the gale
Flew like a bird; and far and fast the wreathèd stem*
    did sail
Till with the morn's first hour the land broke on the
    sailor's sight,

* See Note C.

The headlands great and mountains steep and sea-cliffs
    shining bright.
  The voyage ended straightway sprang the Weder
    folk ashore;
Made fast the ship, and shook abroad their corslets
    and war-store,
Thankful to God that He had made so smooth their
    watery way.
  Then from the cliff the Scyldings' guard, the watcher
    of the bay,
Saw bright shields o'er the bulwarks borne and war-
    gear shaken free,
And much he wondered in his thought to know who
    these might be.
Borne on his horse did Hrothgar's thane draw nigh
    unto the beach,
His strong spear quiv'ring in his hands, and thus with
    measured speech
He said: "What men be ye who thus, full-armed and
    clad in mail,
Across the sea-ways and the waves in tall ship hither
    sail?
Here by the shore my watch I keep, that never foe
    may shame
Nor with their shipmen scathe the land of Danes. But
    never came
More openly shield-bearing men! No leave of kin
    have ye,
Nor warrior's password do ye know! Yet never did
    I see

A greater earl upon the earth than yonder armèd lord;
No common man is he, but one made glorious by his
 sword
Unless his face and noble presence lie! Now must I
 know
Both who ye are and whence ye come ere ye may
 farther go,
Unhindered guests in Danish land. Sea-wanderers
 from afar
Hear my plain words; and, haste is best, say who and
 whence ye are."
 Thus did the eldest answer him—the leader of the
 band
Unlocked his word-hoard: "We are folk of Gothic
 kin and land,
And hearthmates true of Higelac. Far was my father's
 fame
Spread through the world, a highborn chief, and Ecg-
 theow was his name.
Ere, full of days, he passed from hall, he many a year
 did bide,
And him wise men remember well in all the world so
 wide.
Now Halfdene's son, the people's guard, thy lord, we
 come to see
With friendly mind. O be to us a kindly guide!
 For we
Before the mighty lord of Danes a mickle errand bring.
Nor shall my inmost thought be hid; thou know'st if
 true the thing

We've heard for sooth, that in dark night some bitter
    secret foe,
I wot not what ill-doer, bringeth dread and unknown
    woe
And shame and death on Scylding folk; and I with
    counsel free
May teach to Hrothgar, wise and good, to win the
    victory;
That so from him this baleful grief for ever may be
    rolled,
And happiness come back when these heart-burning
    waves are cold;
Else must he thole sore straits for aye, and trouble
    while on high
He sits in stately hall!"
                      Then did the fearless thane reply,
The warder as on steed he sat: "He who can rightly
    rede,
The wise shield-warrior, must judge of every word and
    deed.
Doubtless ye come, a friendly band, to see the
    Scyldings' lord—
Pass on, with me your guide, and bear the battle-
    weed and sword!
And I will bid my kinsmen thanes to guard from
    every foe
Your new-tarred ship here on the sand, till she again
    shall go
With wreathèd neck o'er seas and bear your chief to
    Wederland.

Safe may he be in battle stress who manfully shall
    stand!"
  The ship, wide-bosomed, on the waves there fast
    at anchor rode,
And forth they went. The boar above their plated
    helmets glowed—
The guarding boar, bedecked with gold, fire-hardened,
    many-hued.*
Together moving on they strode, right fierce their
    warlike mood,
Until the hall, all glorious wrought with gold, they
    could espy
Where Hrothgar dwelt. The goodliest hall it was
    beneath the sky
'Mong dwellers on the earth; and light wide o'er
    the land it gave.
And then the warrior showed them clear that palace
    of the brave
That thither they might take their way; then turned
    his horse and spake:
"'Tis time for me to leave you here. In all ye
    undertake
The Almighty Father keep you safe and give you
    honour due!
Down to the shore must I, to guard 'gainst any
    foeman's crew."
The stone-paved street, of many hues, together led
    them on;
Clashed bright steel rings in shirt of mail, and hand-
    locked corselet shone,

        * See Note D.

As in their dread array they went right onward to the hall.
Broad shield and buckler hard they laid, sea-weary, 'gainst the wall;
Their spears, with shafts of ashen grey, the seamen's arms, stood near;
When on the bench they sat them down rang mail and battle-gear;
Well weaponed were these ironsides.*

       Hard by a knight did stand
And haughtily these warriors asked their kinship and their land:
"Whence come ye with these plated shields, grey war-shirts, helmets high,
And sheaf of battle-spears? Herald, and Hrothgar's thane am I.
A prouder band of outland men I never yet have seen;
No outcasts hither do ye come; but all for pride I ween
And in the glory of your hearts have ye sought Hrothgar now!"
Then answered high the Gothic chief and stern his helmèd brow:
"Board-mates of Higelac are we. Beowulf is my name.
Before thy lord, great Halfdene's son, will I my errand frame

---

* 'Ironsides.' I borrow this happy rendering of *íren préát* from Mr. Arnold.

If greeting we may bring to him for he is kind and
    good."
  Wulfgar, (the Wendels' chief was he, well known
    to all his mood,
His wisdom and his worth), replied: "According
    to thy prayer
Before the Scyldings' lord, the Danes' ring-giver, will
    I bear
The tidings of thy coming here, and quickly answer
    bring
As that good lord thinks meet to give."
                           Then went he where the king
Was sitting, old and hoary-haired, amid his troop
    of thanes.
Stately he moved until he stood beside the lord of
    Danes,
(Knowing the seemly ways of courts), and to his chief
    thus spoke:
"From far across the watery ways have come some
    Gothic folk;
Their chief these warriors call by name Beowulf; and
    they pray
That they may speak with thee my lord! Do not
    thou say them nay,
Kind Hrothgar! They may vie with earls in comely
    battle-weed,
And he who leads these warriors here right worthy is
    indeed."
  Then Hrothgar spoke, the Scyldings' aid: "I knew
    him as a boy;

Ecgtheow his sire was called; to him Hrethel the
    Goth with joy
His only daughter gave to wife; now hither comes
    his heir
To seek a kindly friend! 'Twas said by seamen who
    did bear
Thank-offerings yonder to the Goths, that in his
    hand-grip lay
The mighty strength of thirty men. I ween for help
    and stay
'Gainst Grendel's wrath has holy God to us Danes
    sent him now;
And for the greatness of his heart rich gifts will I
    allow.
Haste! Bid them in and see us here together
    kindred thanes—
And say moreover that they come right welcome to
    the Danes."
  Forth from the hall then Wulfgar went. "My
    glorious lord," said he,
"The East-Danes' ruler, bids me say he knows thy
    ancestry;
And welcome hither do ye come, ye warriors o'er the
    wave!
Now go ye in and Hrothgar see, in helm and war-
    gear brave,
But here let shields and deadly shafts the end of
    speech abide."
  Up rose the chief amid his knights, a band of
    warriors tried;

To guard the weapons some remained, obedient to their head,
The rest together hastened on, by Wulfgar's guidance led,
Below the roof of Heorot's hall; nor paused the hero good
Till stern beneath his helmèd brow he on the dais stood.*
Then while his mail, by smith-craft wrought, and hauberk glittered bright,
Beowulf spoke: "To Hrothgar hail! The kinsman and the knight
Of Higelac am I; great deeds I've many done in youth.
Now in my native land to me the tidings came for sooth
Of Grendel's work. Seafaring men have said that this fair hall,
This best of dwellings, idle stands, and to your warriors all
Useless when 'neath the vault of heaven the evening light is hid.
And me my folk, the best of them, wise churls, have earnest bid
To seek thee now, O Hrothgar, lord! they know my strength and might;
Blood-reddened have they seen me come from foemen in the fight,
There bound I monsters, Eotens crushed, and slew within the wave

* See Note E.

The Nicors of the night; dreed pain; but quelled the
    foe and gave
Requital for the wrongs and woes that Weder folk
    had tholed.
  And now with Grendel, with the fiend, the monster
    will I hold
Combat alone. O Scyldings' lord! O ruler of Bright
    Danes!
I ask of thee this only boon—that thou, O shield of
    thanes!
Kind lord of men! wilt not forbid, now I have come
    thus far,
That with my band of earls alone—these valiant men
    of war—
I may make Heorot clean.
                Yet more! I've heard, so bold is he,
Weapons the monster heedeth not, and therefore (so
    on me
May Higelac my lord look blithe!) in fight I scorn
    to bear
Broad shield or yellow targe or sword; but with my
    handgrip fair
I'll clutch the fiend and seek his life—foeman alone
    'gainst foe—
And he whom death shall take away the doom of God
    shall know!
  If he shall conquer, unaffrayed will he—I know it
    well—
In this war-hall the Goths devour as oft on Danes he
    fell;*

    * 'Danes' here in the original *Hréðmen*.

Then if death taketh me thou wilt not need to hide my head :—*

Grendel will have me, drenched in gore; my bleeding body, dead,

He'll bear away in hope of feast; the fiend who walks alone

Will ruthless eat,—the moorland wide shall be my burial stone!

Not long for me thy kindly cares! But if in war I fail

Send Higelac my battle-weed, this goodly shirt of mail,

That guards my breast. 'Tis Hrethel's gift, and 'twas by Wayland made.

Weird ever goeth as she must!"

                  Then spoke the Scyldings' aid :

"Thou com'st to us, Beowulf friend! for honour 'gainst the foe;

Great was the fight thy father fought, who Hatholaf laid low

'Mong Wylfings, when the Weder-kin refused him for their head;

Thence to the Danes, the Scylding folk, o'er heaving seas he sped,

When first in youth I ruled the Danes, and swayed the kingdom wide

And treasure-hold of men. Ere then my Heregar had died,

My elder brother, Halfdene's son—a better man than me!

        * *i.e.* 'bury me.' See Note F.

And then with gifts I healed the feud, and o'er the
 broad-backed sea
Send to the Wylfing treasures good and bound him
 fast by oaths.
 To tell the tale to any man is grief my spirit
 loathes,
The shame and deadly scathe that Grendel's evil
 heart has done
To Heorŏt and to me! My thanes are minished, one
 by one;
By Grendel's horror Weird has swept the warrior band
 away.
 Yet that proud monster from his work God easily
 can stay!
 Over their ale-cups many a time they boasted—
 drunk with beer—
These mighty men, that they would bide, within the
 mead-hall here,
With sharp-edged swords for Grendel's raid, and at
 the morning tide
When daylight broke, this lordly house was seen with
 blood all dyed,
The blood of slaughter in the hall—the benches
 steeped with gore—
Fewer my faithful knights beloved, and death had
 taken more!
 Sit now to meat thou famed in war! and to thy
 heart's content
Take thou thine ease."
          Together then the Gothic warriors went,

And on the bench prepared for them in hall, in all
    their pride
They sat them down—the bold of heart. A thane
    their needs supplied
Who bore a flagon goodly chased and poured the
    brewage clear;
And sweet the while was minstrel's song, and joyous
    was the cheer
Of Danes and Goths in Heorot there, a goodly
    company.

IV.

HUNFERD AND BEOWULF.

Hunferd the son of Ecglaf spoke—at Hrothgar's
    feet sat he—
And thus let loose his secret grudge; (for much did
    him displease
The coming of Beowulf now—bold sailor o'er the seas.
To none on earth would he allow a greater fame
    'mong men
Beneath the heavens than his): "Art thou the same
    Beowulf then,
Who swam a match with Breca once upon the waters
    wide,
When ye vainglorious searched the waves, and risked
    your lives for pride

Upon the deep? Nor hinder you could any friend
    or foe
From that sad venture. Then ye twain did on the
    waters row;
Ye stretched your arms upon the flood; the sea-ways
    ye did mete;
O'er billows glided—with your hands them tossed—
    though fiercely beat
The rolling tides and wintry waves! Seven nights
    long toilèd ye
In waters' might; but Breca won—he stronger was
    than thee!
And to the Hathoræms * at morn washed shoreward
    by the flood,
Thence his loved native land he sought—the Brond-
    ings' country good,
And stronghold fair, where he was lord of folk and
    burg and rings.
Right well 'gainst thee his vaunt he kept. But yet
    I ween worse things
May now befall thee, (doughtily as thou in shocks
    of fight
Hast ever done), if thou dar'st bide near Grendel for
    a night!"

 Beowulf spoke: "Lo! many things, friend Hunferd,
    drunk with beer,
Thou tell'st of Breca and his deed! The truth now
    shalt thou hear,

* The inhabitants of that part of Norway called formerly
Raumaríki, now Romsdal.

That I was stronger 'mong the waves,—more steadfast in the flood,
Than any man. When we were boys, we spoke in boyish mood,
And in the deep to risk our lives did one another dare.
And so 'twas done. When out we swam our firm-grasped swords were bare
To guard ourselves from water-beasts; and nowise could he swim
Swifter than me, or float away; nor would I part from him.
Together thus for five nights long upon the deep were we,
Till coldest weather, northern wind, dark night, and stormy sea
Beat fiercely, and the surging flood us sundered. Rough the wave!
Wrathful the water-beasts! But help my hard-wov'n hauberk gave
Against their rage; the broidered war-shirt lay upon my breast
All golden wrought. With deadly hate a foe in fast clutch pressed
And to the bottom dragged me down; yet with my battle-brand,
I stabbed the monster through—such hap was mine—and by my hand
In shock of fight the mighty sea-beast died.
       Yet on me still

Crowded unceasingly and fierce the workers of all ill.
With my good sword I smote them hard as meet it was to do:
No joy of feast ill-workers had though me for food they threw
To bottom of the sea; but all smitten with sword, they lay
Cast up in heaps upon the beach dead at the break of day,*
Never again to stop the path of sailors through the deep!
Dawned in the east God's beacon bright,—the waves were lulled to sleep,
And I beheld the windy walls—the headlands of the sea.
Weird helpeth oft the earl undoomed who battles manfully!
Nine Nicors with my sword I slew—such hap to me was given;
Never by night was harder fight beneath the vault of heaven;
Never was man more sore beset upon the stormy wave;
Yet thus my life from grip of foes did I, though wearied, save.
The flood-tide then and heaving sea cast me on Finnish land.
  Nought did I ever hear of thee, nor terrors of thy brand,

* See Note G.

In such fierce fight.   Not Breca—no ! nor thou—in
    battle-play
With blood-stained swords e'er wrought a deed (nor
    great the boast I say)
So doughtily, though by thy hand thy chiefs, thy
    brethren, fell!
And, spite of all thy wit, for them thou'lt dree the
    pains of hell!
For, Ecglaf's son! I tell thee truth, that Grendel
    ne'er had wrought
So many sorrows on thy lord, nor shame on Heorot
    brought,
If that thy mind and heart were stout as thou dost
    say they are.
But well he knows he hath no need to fear the clash
    of war,
Or hatred of thy folk and thee—'victorious Scyldings'
    hight!
He seizeth pledge, he spareth none, but as he lists to
    fight,
Or sleep, or eat, he recketh not of all the Gar-Danes'
    wrath ;
Soon shall he know the strength in war and valour
    of a Goth!
Then to the mead-feast afterward glad let him go
    who may,
When on the sons of men shall dawn the morrow
    of that day,
And from the south the sun shall shine with beams
    of glory clad ! "

The treasure-giver hoary-haired, the bold in war, was glad;
When thus Beowulf's steadfast mind the Bright-Dane's ruler heard
He knew his help assured. There then 'mong warriors laughter stirred,
And music sounded; speech was sweet; and forth then Waltheow came,
The queen of Hrothgar, decked with gold. Mindful of kin and name
She greeted all the men in hall, and to the East-Danes' lord
Joyful she gave the beaker first, and pledged him at the board
Dear to his folk and blithe of heart. And glad the valiant king
Partook of feast and banquet-cup; the while around the ring
Of warriors old and youthful knights the Helmings lady passed;*
To each she gave the goblet rich till by good hap at last
The necklaced queen with courtly grace before Beowulf trod,
Gave him the mead-cup, greeted him, and offered thanks to God
In seemly words, that He had given her heart's desire indeed

* 'Helmings' the people of Helm, who, in the Traveller's song (29), is said to have ruled the Wylfings. See p. 22

To find an earl whom she could trust to help them in
    their need.
  From Waltheow's hands he took the cup, the warrior
    fierce in fight,
And, stirred in spirit for the fray, ordered his words
    aright,
And thus the son of Ecgtheow spoke: "When with
    my warrior band
I trod my ship and put to sea, strong did my purpose
    stand
Throughly to work thy people's will, or else a corse
    to lie
Fast in the foeman's gripe. And earl-like now that
    deed will I
Make perfect, or in this mead-hall my end of days
    abide!"
  Well pleased the lady heard the speech, Beowulf's
    words of pride,
And decked with gold, the people's queen sat joyous
    by her lord.
Then in the hall, as oft before, was spoken bravest word,
The noise of an exultant folk, and men were full of glee
Till Halfdene's son sought nightly rest. He knew
    that war must be
With that fell monster in the hall [where they could
    safely bide
Only]* while they could see the sun, till over all
    should glide,

  * A line seems to have dropped out here. In the words within brackets I have followed Grein's conjecture.

Wan 'neath the clouds, the dusky night, the shadow-helm of men.
  Uprose the sitters all; the king with ordered words again
Greeted Beowulf; gave to him the hall in charge to hold,
And said: "To no man ever yet have I this house of gold
Entrusted save to thee, since first I hand and shield could raise.
Have now and keep this best of halls! Think of thy deeds of praise,
Make known thy strength, watch 'gainst the foe! And nothing shalt thou lack
If from this glorious work of thine alive thou comest back!"
  Then from the hall amid his knights forth passed the Scyldings' head,
The warrior-lord Queen Waltheow sought, the partner of his bed.

V.

THE FIGHT WITH GRENDEL.

'Gainst Grendel had the glorious king—so were the people told—
A hall-guard set; an eoten-watch its special post to hold
Around the lord of Danes.
                      His trust the Gothic chief did place
Surely in strength of his great soul, and in th' Almighty's grace.
He doffed his iron coat of mail, the helmet from his brow;
His goodly sword of choicest steel he gave his thane; and now
He bade him keep his fighting gear; and ere he climbed his bed
The valiant Goth Beowulf thus his words of vaunting said:
"No meaner man I count myself in warlike deeds and might
Than Grendel; therefore (though I may) with sword I will not smite
Nor take his life. With these good arms he knoweth not to kill,
Nor hew the shield, though proud he be of all his deadly skill!

We two this night shall use no sword, if weaponless
    he dare
The battle seek. To either then—however it may
    fare—
Shall God all-knowing glory give as shall to Him seem
    best."
  He laid him down, the brave in war, his cheek
    the bolster pressed;
And round him in the hall asleep lay many a seaman
    bold.
No man among them thought again his kinsfolk to
    behold,
Or dear loved home,—the lordly burg where he was
    born and bred;
Already in the hall they knew too many Danes were
    dead!
But God for them wove victory,* and gave them help
    and joy,
That by the strength of one alone their foe they should
    destroy;
For sooth is known that mighty God mankind hath
    ever swayed.
  Then through the darksome night came prowling
    he who walks in shade.
The fighters slept who were to keep the many-pointed
    hall,

---

* *Ac him dryhten forgeaf wígspéda gewiofu.* The phrase, Grimm remarks, is purely heathen, 'God' being only substituted for 'Weird.' (D. M. p. 387.)

All slept save one. To men 'twas known that on
    them might not fall,
Since God forbade, that fiend in gloom. With wrath-
    ful courage high
Beowulf waited for the foe the battle-doom to try.
  Down from the moor, 'neath misty fells, bearing the
    wrath of God,
Thinking in that high hall to snare some sleeper, Gren-
    del trod.
Onward he went beneath the clouds, until he could
    behold
The goodly-plated house of men, the heroes' hall of
    gold.
Not now first sought he Hrothgar's home, but never
    had he yet
In all his life's-day such hall-thanes or harder warriors
    met!
Accursed to the house he strode; and soon beneath
    his hands
The door flew open at his touch though closed with
    fire-wrought bands.
With thoughts of ill he angry burst within the open door,
And straightway trod with wrathful steps the many-
    coloured floor,
While from his eyes like flame of fire forth flashed a
    baleful light!
  Together in the hall he saw, all sleeping, many a
    knight;
A crowd of kindred men. The evil monster laughed
    in heart,

And thought that ere the dawning day body and life
    he'd part
In all of them, for greedily he weened of plenteous
    meat.
But doomed had Weird that from that night man's
    flesh he ne'er should eat.
Then earnestly Beowulf watched how with his dreadful
    grasp
The wicked scather wrought his will. He paused not,
    in his clasp,
For first adventure, swift he seized and slew a sleeping
    thane;
Bit in the flesh, gulped mouthfuls down, drank blood
    from every vein,
And soon the corse was all devoured even to the hands
    and feet,
  Nearer he drew and felt Beowulf lying on the seat;—
The fiend made one fierce clutch at him, but propped
    upon his arm
Swift did Beowulf seize the wretch, and soon that lord
    of harm
Found that in all realms of earth he ne'er before had
    met
In any man so strong a grip, and fears his heart
    beset.
But not for that could he break loose. His mind was
    bent on flight,
To seek his noisy devildom, and flee into the night;
Work like to this in his life's-day he ne'er before had
    tried!

Bethought him then Beowulf of his words at even-
   tide;
Upright he sprang with tightened grip, even till his
   fingers bled,
Close following the fiend outside when from the house
   he fled.
The monster cast about in thought how he might far-
   ther go
And seek the mere amid the fens—he knew that grasp
   of foe
Held fast his fingers' strength. His path a bitter end
   had found
At Heorot! Loudly the lordly hall re-echoed to the
   sound!
To every Dane who dwelt in burg—to boldest warriors
   all—
The ale seemed savourless, so fierce the fighting in the
   hall.
   Great wonder was that hall of men these fighters'
   rage withstood,
And that it fell not to the ground, that dwelling strong
   and good;
But all within it and without 'twas strengthened 'gainst
   that day
By iron bands forged cunningly. Yet from the sills,
   men say,
Was many a gilded mead-bench torn where those dread
   foemen fought.
The wisest Scyldings little weened that house, so goodly
   wrought

With horn of hart, would e'er be loosed, or in men's
 strife be broke,
Save when the outstretched arms of fire should swallow
 it in smoke!
 Uprose the cry again renewed; and at the sound
 did fall
An eerie dread on every Dane who listened from the
 wall,
And heard the enemy of God his shriek of horror yell,
Not glory's song, the bitter wail of that bond-slave of
 hell.
Fast was he held by him to whom the greatest might
 was given
Of all men in this day of life. For nothing under
 heaven
Would he, the shield of earls, alive that murderer let
 loose,
Nor counted he his own life's-day to any folk of use.
 Then many of Beowulf's earls unsheathed the good
 old sword
To save the life, if so they might, of their great prince
 and lord.
They knew it not, these fighters keen, when mingling
 in the fray,
Thinking to hew about them well and tear the soul
 away,
That not the choicest blade on earth nor war-bill e'er
 could bite
That scather foul; but edge of sword and every
 weapon bright

Beowulf had forsworn. Yet doomed this day to wretched end
Was that bad sprite, and in the power of devils far to wend!
The foe of God, who oft before in mirthful mood had wrought
Mischief upon mankind, now found his body served him nought;
Still of his hand the valiant thane of Higelac kept hold.
Hateful to each the other's life: sore pangs the monster tholed;
Soon on his shoulder yawned a wound, atwain sprang sinews riven,
Sundered was flesh—and joy of war was to Beowulf given!
  Wounded to death must Grendel flee, and seek his joyless home
Beneath the shelter of the fens; life's-end he knew was come,
And told was all his tale of days!
                           And thus in bloody war
The Danes' desires were all fulfilled; for he who came from afar,
The wise and brave, had cleansed the hall, and saved from shock of foes;
Glad of his night-work now was he and doughty deeds! The woes,
The grief of heart that erst they dreed, by bitter need compelled—
The sorrows of the Danes—were soothed, for well had he upheld,

The Gothic chief, his vaunting bold. That was the
    token fair
When down the warrior flung the hand and arm and
    shoulder there,
And all together Grendel's gripe lay neath the lofty
    roof.

VI.

THE PURSUIT OF GRENDEL.

Round the gift-hall I've heard it told came many
    men of war,
And o'er wide ways at morning-tide came chieftains
    near and far,
To gaze upon that wondrous thing the foe had left
    behind.
And no man sorrowed for his death of those who
    went to find
How wearily the vanquished fiend thence, overcome
    in fight,
Took his last steps to Nicor's mere, death-doomed
    and put to flight.
Blood mingled with the troubled waves—the gloomy
    waters rolled
Hot with the gore of him, death-doomed, soon as
    in that fen-hold

Sundered from bliss, by hell received, his heathen
    spirit fled.
  Then from the mere they homeward now their
    gladsome journey sped,
The band of warriors old and young—white was each
    hero's steed,
Proudly their horses they bestrode; and of Beowulf's
    deed
Was spoken much; and oft 'twas said that o'er this
    great wide earth,
By the two seas,* or south or north, was none of
    higher worth
'Mong shielded men beneath the sky, nor worthier
    to be king.
Yet nowise surely would they blame their lord in
    anything,
Their Hrothgar kind—good king was he!
                         Sometimes their horses dun,
Of choicest breed, these warriors made to leap and
    races run,
Where'er the meadow paths seemed fair.
                            Sometimes with ready lore
Would Hrothgar's thane, who many a tale could tell
    of days of yore,
With high thoughts laden, shape the truth in ordered
    words aright;
And deftly would he then begin to sing Beowulf's
    might,
And skilfully to weave the tale with other stories told

      * The Baltic and the German Ocean.

Of Sigmund and his glorious deeds, 'the Wælsings fighting bold—
Far travels—wonders many—feuds and crimes—that no man knew
Save Fitela, his sister's son, in war his comrade true.
Full many of the Eoten race their swords had beaten down;
And Sigmund's name, his death-day o'er, was mighty of renown,
For he had slain—the brave in war!—the worm that kept the hoard.
'Neath the grey rock that daring deed alone the highborn lord
Had wrought; no Fitela was there; yet so did it befall
His sword went through the wondrous worm, and struck against the wall,
And dead the dragon lay! The glorious chief had done the feat
That he the ring-hoard might enjoy as to himself seemed meet.
A ship he loaded—to her lap he bore the shining freight;
And fire consumed the worm. In glorious deeds was none so great
'Mong wanderers all the nations through as he, the warrior's shield.
Thus long ago he throve.*

Thereafter Heremod did yield

* See Note H.

The warfare and the power and might, and 'mong
  the Jutes betrayed
Was quickly given to foeman's hands; on him long
  woes were laid;
To all his nobles and his folk a life-long care was he;
And oft wise churls in earlier times bewailed the
  venture free
Of that stout-hearted one to whom they looked for
  help at need;
Hoping the son of kings should thrive, to father's
  rights succeed,
And keep the folk the hoard and burg, the Scyldings'
  native land,
And heroes' realm. The guilt was his! Whereas
  Beowulf's hand
Was trustier far to all mankind and friends!'
                                    And thus the while
Racing upon their steeds did they the yellow path
  beguile.

VII.

THE REJOICINGS AT HEOROT.

Now worn away was morning light while flocked stout-hearted men
There in the lofty house that they the wondrous thing might ken.
From bride-bower * forth the King himself, for virtues high renowned,
Came glorious, lord of hoarded rings, with all his nobles round;
And with him o'er the mead-path trod, among her maids, the Queen.
Into the hall he went and stood the pillars high between;
On Grendel's arm he looked, and on the steep roof gilded bright,
And said: "Let thanks be given to God forthwith for this blest sight!
Much trouble have I undergone and grief at Grendel's hand;
But wonders upon wonders aye are wrought at God's command.
Not long ago no hope had I of comfort in my woe

* '*Brýd-búr*,' the dwelling-house of the king and probably of his personal attendants.

Through life's long days, when this fair hall with gore
    and blood did flow;
And sorrows wrung my Witan all; from devil, foe,
    and sprite
This stronghold of the folk they wist not how to
    guard aright.
Now in the strength of God a man the mighty deed
    has wrought
Which hitherto we could not do with all our wisest
    thought.
Lo! she may say—if yet she lives, the maid who
    bore such son
Among mankind—that in her travail God has kindly
    done!
And now Beowulf, best of men! I'll love thee while
    I live
Ev'n as a son. Our new-made bond hold fast! All
    I can give
Of worldly joys thou shalt not lack. Full oft have
    I for less
Reward and hoarded treasure dealt to warriors worse
    in stress;
Thy glory by the deeds thou'st done shall live for
    evermore,
And may th' Almighty do thee good as He has done
    before!"
  Then spake Beowulf, Ecgtheow's son: "Right
    willingly this feat
Did we perform, and stout of heart the monster's
    power did meet.

Yet would I rather thou thyself hadst seen in all his pride
The fallen foe. I thought to have him fast in fetters tied,
On death-bed struggling for his life, within my hand-grip laid,
And not that he should 'scape! But hinder him, since God forbade,
I could not; all too weak my grasp to hold the deadly foe!
Too strong was he upon his feet. Yet here did he forego
His life's defence, and left his shoulder, hand, and arm behind;
Small comfort has he bought withal—most wretched of mankind!
Not longer shall he live for that—sin-laden, working ill—
Pangs hold him fast in deadly grasp, bale's fetters he doth fill,
And there all stained with guilt must he the awful doom abide
As the Creator glorious shall unto him decide."
 More silent then was Ecglaf's son,[*] no vaunting words spake he
Of warlike deeds, when pressing forward nobles all could see
On the high roof the fingers dread won by Beowulf's might.

[*] Hunferd.

A hideous prong most like to steel—hand-spur of
    heathen knight—
Was each hard finger-nail. Men said no iron e'er
    so good
Could pierce or hurt that deadly hand now all with
    gore imbrued.
  'Twas bidden soon that Heort within should be made
    fair again,
And men and women many were who decked that
    house of men,
The hall of guests. Along the walls shone hangings
    wrought with gold—
Sight wondrous fair to any man who may the like
    behold!
Yet shattered was the glorious house, within though
    iron bound,
The hinges torn away—the roof alone unhurt was
    found,
When stained with deeds of guilt the fiend, of life
    despairing, fled.
  Try it who will—not easily the flight from death
    is sped!
Needs must the sons of men, soul-bearing, here who
    earth do keep,
Seek place prepared where close in grave their bodies
    aye shall sleep.
  Now was it time and tide when Halfdene's son to
    hall should go;
The King himself would taste the feast. Nor ever
    did I know

Of folk in greater throng who better stood around their lord,
And happily, of banquet glad, down sat they to the board.
Full many a cup of mead they drank with joy in that high hall,
Hrothgar and Hrothulf, kinsmen brave. Within was Heorot all
Filled full of friends—for hitherto no wrong had Scyldings done.
  Then to Beowulf Hrothgar gave the prize of battle won,
A golden crest, a banner bright, a great and goodly sword,
And helm and corselet; many saw them borne before the lord.
Beowulf quaffed the cup in hall; before the warriors now
No need had he to blush for gifts! Did never men I trow
To others at the mead-bench give four treasures, dight with gold,
In friendlier wise. With wires around the helmet's top was rolled
A boss* outside to guard the head, that in the press of fight
Should never sword, though bright and keen, the shielded warrior bite.

* *Wala.* The precise meaning of this word is uncertain; it may have been a crest of some kind, or the framework on the helmet. See Note D.

Within the hall the lord of earls bade lead upon the floor
Eight steeds with head-stalls plated fair: and one a saddle bore
Dyed cunningly, enriched with wealth, the high-king's battle-seat,
When Halfdene's son would sword-play try. And never knew defeat
The far-famed one in front of war where thickest lay the dead.
  Then did the Ingwines'* prince give o'er both steeds and weapons dread
Into Beowulf's hands, and bid him joy in them to have.
Thus manlike did the mighty prince, hoard-warden of the brave,
With steeds and treasure well repay the deadly shocks of fight.
On such let no man e'er cast blame who truth will speak aright!
  Yet more, to every man who with Beowulf crossed the wave
On mead-bench there the lord of earls rich gifts and heirlooms gave;
And bade the gold be paid for him whom Grendel foully slew,
As more he would have slain save that Beowulf's valour true,

* 'Ingwines,' the Danes—*proximi oceano Ingævones.* (Tacitus, Ger. 2.)

And God all-knowing, Weird withstood; for over all
　　mankind
God ruled as even now He doth; and that to bear in
　　mind
With forethought wise is ever best; for much of joy
　　and woe
He who on earth abideth long through days of life
　　must know.
　Along the mead-bench song and shout together
　　mingled rang,
And Hrothgar's bard, to sound of harp, the oft-told
　　story sang—
The joy of hall—how Halfdene's knight smote down
　　the sons of Finn.

The Bard's Tale.

Hnæf the Scylding, Halfdene's thane, in Friesvale
　　dying lay.
The faith of Jutes had Hildeburh no need to praise
　　that day,
Guiltless bereft—sad lady she!—of sons and brothers
　　dear
By bitter fate, in shield-play there pierced by the cruel
　　spear!
No causeless tears at God's decree did Hoka's daughter
　　shed,
When morning dawned, and she beheld her kinsmen
　　lying dead
Beneath the light of day—men once her dearest joy
　　in life!

Yet slaughtered were the thanes of Finn, but few outlived the strife;
No whit could they 'gainst Hengest's might maintain the battle-field
Nor hope from him, by fighting fierce, that remnant sad to shield;
And therefore did they offer peace; they promised to prepare
For Hengest's self another court with hall and high-seat fair;
There with the son of Jutes to halve the power; and every day,
When gifts were dealt, should Folkvald's son * to Danes meet honour pay,
And bracelets give to Hengest's band, and wealth, and plated gold,
Even like as to his Frisian kin he in the beer-hall told.
  Then fast they made the bond of peace, and sure on either side;
And Finn with oaths to Hengest bound the Witan to provide
With honour for his remnant sad; and that no man should break
By word or deed the bond; nor peace with base thoughts idle make,
Though, lordless now, the Danish men, compelled by bitter need,
Followed the slayer of their chief. And of the murderous deed

* Finn.

If any Frisian e'er should speak with rash and biting word,
Dire vengeance should be meted out on him with edge of sword.
   Sworn was the oath; and from the hoard was brought the treasure bright,
And on the funeral pile they laid the best and bravest knight
In all the Scylding host. Then might ye see beside the pyre
Blood-reddened mail, and golden boar, and helm made hard by fire,
And many a chief with ghastly wounds—the men whom death laid low.
And on Hnæf's pyre did Hildeburh bid in the raging glow
The bodies of her sons be laid for fire to burn away.
The hapless lady them beside, with many a mourning lay,
· Lamented sore. Then rose the smoke, and soaring to the sky,
With roarings loud, above the mound, up-blazed the death-flames high;
Melted the heads—the wound-gates burst—forth did the blood outspring.
From gashes fell in every corse; and fire, the greediest thing,
Swallowed death's spoil of either folk—the strength of both was spent!

Of friends bereft, to see the land, then hence the warriors went—
Friesland to see—high burg and homes. But Hengest dwelt with Finn
That bloody winter undisturbed. Yet thought he of his kin
Though o'er the deep he might not drive the ringed stem of his ship.
The sea boiled stormy lashed with wind; icebound in winter's grip
The waters lay; till grange and farm beheld another year,
As still the bliss-bestower comes—the weather glorious-clear—
And winter fled; the lap of earth was fair. The rover guest
Longed from the thorpes to take his way; but rather was his breast
With vengeful thoughts than seafare filled, if yet the bloody deed
He purposed he might throughly work.
      The doom to man decreed
Finn nowise 'scaped when in his heart the heir of Hunlaf laid
The battle-flame, the best of swords—well known 'mong Jutes the blade!
 Thus in his turn by slaughter dire at home fell Finn the bold;
Their voyage o'er when mournfully Guthlaf and Oslaf told

Of struggle fierce, and upon him did all their sorrows lay,
No longer might within his breast the wavering spirit stay.*
With foemen's lives the hall was dight—king Finn in court lay slain—
The Queen was borne away; and hence the bowmen of the Dane
Took to their ships all household gear, each rare and precious thing,
Whate'er in Finn's home they could find belonging to the king;
And o'er the sea-ways to the Danes the noble lady bore
And led her to her folk." †

Sung was the lay, the gleeman's tale; then sport arose, and mirth
Grew loud-voiced on the benches there. From jars of wondrous worth
Cupbearers poured the wine. Then forth came Waltheow, crowned with gold,
Where sat together kinsman twain (for peace they still did hold—
Each to the other faithful yet).‡ Hunferd the speechman too

---

* The meaning of this, I think, is that Guthlaf and Oslaf, having sailed away and gone home, leaving Hengest with Finn, were telling their story at the very time when Finn was dying.

† See Note I.

‡ Hrothgar and his nephew Hrothulf. See p. 47.

Was sitting there at Hrothgar's feet, his heart all men
    deemed true,
And spirit great, though ne'er to kinsmen staunch in
    play of sword.
    The lady of the Scyldings spoke: "Giver of fee!
    My lord!
Take now this cup. All hail to thee, thou kindly
    friend of men!
Speak to the Goths with gentle words as man should
    do; and then,
Mindful of gifts, be good to them. Peace far and
    near is won!
'Twas said to me that thou wast pleased to call the
    knight thy son.
Heorot is cleansed, the bright ring-hall; use well the
    gifts in store
While yet thou may'st, and to thy sons give folk and
    kingdom o'er
When thou must forth to see the Lord! My
    Hrothulf kind I know
With honour will uphold the youths if thou, ere he
    must go,
O Scyldings' friend! shalt leave the world. With
    good will he repay
Our heirs I ween if he remembers all in childhood's day
That we have done to honour him in glory and
    delights." *
    Then turned she to the bench where sat together
    youthful knights;

    * See Note K.

Hrethric and Hrothmund, her two sons, were there and by the twain
Beowulf sat, the glorious Goth. To him with greeting fain
And friendly words the cup was borne; and wrought gold given free—
Two armlets, raiment, rings, and necklace goodliest to see
That e'er I heard of on the earth. Beneath the light of day
No hero's ornament more fair since Hama bore away
The Brosing collar,* gems, and wealth far to the city bright;
And lasting gain he got thereby in Eormenric's despite.
(And Swerting's nephew, Higelac the Goth, the necklace wore
On his last raid, beneath his banner guarding well the store,
And spoil of war. But Weird him took when in the Frisian feud
All for his pride he met with woe. He bore that jewel good
And precious stones—the glorious prince!—the brimming waters through;
'Neath shield he fell, and life of king, breast-weed and collar too

---

* 'Brosing collar.' A famous jewel in the Gothic legend. Mr. Arnold has collected all the passages on the subject in his Beowulf App., p. 201.

Passed to the hands of Franks, when meaner fighters
    robbed the slain
By lot of war, and Gothic folk lay dead on battle-
    plain.)
  Uprose the noise in hall. Then Waltheow spoke
    before them there:
"O youth! Beowulf dear! Take now with joy this
    ring, and wear
This raiment—people's gifts are they. All hail! and
    thrive thou well!
Shew forth thy might; and to these youths thy know-
    ledge gently tell!
I will remember to repay. Thy deeds so glorious are
Men shall thee praise through life-long days in lands
    both near and far,
Yea, widely as the waves enfold the windy walls of
    earth!
Be whilst thou liv'st a happy prince! I give thee
    gifts of worth.
And to my sons be staunch in deeds—their happiness
    uphold!
Here is each earl to other true, gentle each spirit bold,
Leal to his lord; the thanes at peace; the people all
    prepared.
O men well drunken do my hest!"
                      Then to her seat she fared.
Choice was the feast and men drank wine; they wist
    not Weird aright,
The bitter doom to many an earl decreed. Now came
    the night;

King Hrothgar to his house betook him seeking rest
   in sleep
Earls without number kept the hall, as erst was wont
   to keep.
They cleared the benches from the floor, and over it
   they spread
The beds and bolsters. (Doomed to die one drinker
   sought his bed.*)
War-shield and wooden buckler bright beside their
   heads did lie;
And on the bench o'er every knight was seen his
   helmet high,
His corselet ringed, and glorious spear. Such was
   their custom aye,
Whether on foray or at home, oft ready for the fray
Howe'er their liege lord chanced to need. A noble
   people they!

* This refers to Æschere, slain that night by Grendel's mother.

PART II.
GRENDEL'S MOTHER.

THE ARGUMENT.

Grendel's mother bursts upon the sleepers in the hall and carries off Æschere. The grief of the Danes is renewed, but Beowulf comforts Hrothgar and promises to take revenge. They track the footsteps to the mere in the joyless wood. Beowulf plunges in, and in the cavern beneath the waves slays Grendel's mother. He smites the head from Grendel's body and swims ashore with it. There are great rejoicings at Heorot. Laden with gifts, Beowulf and his men take leave of Hrothgar, and return to their own land, where Beowulf tells the story of his adventures to Higelac.

I.

THE WOMAN OF THE MERE.

Then sank they all to sleep. But one bought dear his evening rest;
As oft befell since that gold hall by Grendel was possessed,
Ill doing, till his end was come, and death came after ill.[1]
'Twas seen and widely known 'mong men that after him lived still—
Long after the fierce battle lived—th' avenger of his blood,
His mother; she, the monstrous hag, upon her woes did brood.
Doomed was she aye in wildered waves and waters cold to dwell,
Since guilty Cain his brother slew, and, with that murder fell
Branded, forsook the joys of men and trod the waste. Thence woke
To life the evil sprites of yore; and Grendel of that folk,

The ravening were-wolf, came. But he at Heorot
   found a man
Who watchful waited for the strife. The monster on
   him ran
In death-grips; but Beowulf knew his God-given
   strength and might,
His glorious gifts, and in the Lord Almighty trusted
   right
For help and comfort; therefore he that sprite of
   hell laid low;
O'erthrew the fiend; and humbled thence did man-
   kind's bitter foe,
Sundered from bliss, go forth to see the dwellings of
   the dead.
Now wroth and greedy sought his dam the doleful
   path to tread,
And for her son's death take revenge. To Heorot
   she drew near,
Where deep in sleep the Ring-Danes lay around the
   hall; and fear
Fell on the earls when Grendel's mother in among
   them burst.
Yet, as the strength of maids to men, so less than at
   the first
The terror was—as warlike rage of women is to
   men,
When banded sword by hammer forged on boar-helm
   smites again
And downright shears with reddened blade! Then
   drawn was keen-edged brand

O'er every bench, and buckler broad was grasped in
many a hand;
No thought for helm or corselet strong when terror-
struck had they!
Discovered now she was in haste, to get unscathed
away,
And, clutching swift an earl, she turned her homeward
to the mere.
By the two seas in all his host to Hrothgar none more
dear
Than the shield-warrior thus in sleep from life and
welfare riven.
  Not there Beowulf then; his bower, after the gifts
were given,
Was elsewhere dight. A cry arose in Heort. With
gore imbrued
The well-known hand she took; and through the
town was grief renewed.
No bargain good for either side that lives of friends
must buy!
  Then did the hoary warrior wise, the king, in sad-
ness lie
Soon as he knew his chiefest thane and dearest friend
was dead.
Beowulf now, the victor knight, swift to the bower
they led;
And forth the high-born warrior went amid his band
of thanes,
Ere daybreak, there where waited till the pious king
of Danes

To see if after woful news God any hope would bring,
And o'er the floor the glorious man (while board and
    bench did ring)
Trod with his troop to greet with words the Ingwines'
    lord aright,
And ask if, for this pressing call, he'd had a peaceful
    night?

"Ask not of peace!" then Hrothgar said, "the
    sorrow is renewed
Of Danish folk. Æschere is dead! the elder brother
    good
Of Yrmenlaf, my counsellor, who knew my inmost
    thought;
My comrade when we guarded well our heads what
    time we fought,
When armies met and boar-helms rang! Even so
    should every knight
Be of the best as Æschere was!
                        The wandering deadly sprite
Has laid her hands on him in Heort,—and whether,
    proud of prey
And glad of feast, the fiend again has ta'en her home-
    ward way
I wot not. She has 'venged the wrong thou didst her
    yester-eve
By Grendel's death in fierce close grips, for that he
    long did grieve
My folk and minished them. In fight he paid his
    forfeit breath!
Now comes the other mighty foe to wreak her off-
    spring's death;

Far hath she carried on the feud; and therefore every
    thane,
Who for his wealth-bestower mourns, must feel heart-
    rending pain:
Low lies the hand that pleasant things gave freely to
    you all!
    The landward dwellers of my folk I've heard, at
    talk in hall,
Saying two such mark-steppers great were known to
    tread the moor;
Foul sprites; the one in woman's shape, as they
    might know most sure;
The other wretch in guise of man trod o'er the out-
    cast ways,
(But bigger he than other men), and him in former
    days
The country-folk did Grendel call. Their sire no man
    can tell,
If ever spirit of the gloom ere them was born. They
    dwell
In hidden places, cliffs wolf-haunted, windy nesses
    steep,
And wild morass, whence to the plain the mountain
    torrents leap
Down from the mist-enfolded hills. Not far away the
    mere,
A mile by measure; o'er it hang the woods, fast-rooted,
    sere,
The waters shrouding; nightly there is seen a wonder
    dread—

Fire on the flood! No son of man with all his skill
may tread
In that abyss; the hart that roams the heath in
antlered pride,
Pressed by the hounds and hunted far, in woody holt
may hide,
But ere he plunge his head therein upon the bank
will die.
A place accurst: the troubled waves heave wan
beneath the sky
When wind upstirreth weather foul, and all the lift
grows dark,
And th' heavens weep.] In thee alone the speech now finds its mark!
Thou know'st not yet the perilous spot, where thou
may'st find the lair
Of this sin-laden monster; go, now seek it if thou
dare!
If from the fight thou comest back I'll give thee
treasures old;
And for reward, as erst I gave, shalt thou have twisted
gold."
Then spake Beowulf, Ecgtheow's son: "O wise
man, sorrow not!
'Tis better to avenge a friend than too much mourn
his lot.
Each one of us must bide the end of life, and what
he may
Of glory win ere death, for so, when life is past
away,

That to the warrior will be best. O kingdom's warder,
   rise!
Hence let us go at once and see where Grendel's
   mother flies.
I promise thee no hiding-place—earth's bosom, or
   deep sea,
Or mountain wood—shall shelter her wherever she
   may flee.
For every sorrow thou this day I ween shalt comfort
   take."
The king sprang up with thanks to God for what
   Beowulf spake.
   Then Hrothgar's horse, the curly-maned, was
      bridled; stately rode
The wise king forth; with him on foot shield-bearing
   warriors strode.
   O'er field, and through the woody glades they
      tracked her footprints sure,
And ever onward as she'd gone, up o'er the murky
   moor,
Bearing, a corse, the noblest knight who guarded
   Hrothgar's hall.
By narrow paths the Ætheling's son climbed up the
   rocky wall,
The ways unknown, the nesses steep, and Nicor-
   haunted ground.
He went in front with watchful men to search the land
   around
Till suddenly the wood accurst he reached; o'er
   boulders grey

Hung mountain trees, and down below dark troubled waters lay.
  Then to the Danes, the Scyldings' friends, was sorrow hard to bear,
A grievous thing to every earl, for on the headland there
They found the head of Æschere; and 'tis said that all the wave
With hot blood seethed. A while the horns a warlike summons gave;
Then all sat down; the serpent brood they watched upon the mere,
Strange sea-drakes swimming, and on rocks the Nicors lying near;
The worms and creatures wild that oft at early noon foreshow
Sad end to those who sail. But when they heard the war-horn blow
Roused by the clang they rushed in rage and bitterness away.
The prince of Goths with bended bow smote one, and sluggish lay,
Sundered from life and watery toil, the creature on the flood,
For deep the hardened arrow-head within the body stood.
The sharp-hooked boarspear from the waves then lightly drew ashore
The wondrous water-beast by force o'ercome and smitten sore:

Men gazed upon the grisly thing.*
                      Now was Beowulf drest
In earl-beseeming weed;—but not of life he recked:
    his breast
Was covered by his mail-shirt strong, hand-woven,
    and diverse hued,
Which now must try the deep, and guard his life in
    grapple rude
And deadly clutch of foe. Upon his head the helmet
    sheen
Must see the bottom of the mere, and search the
    depths between.
Made rich it was with gold and laced with lordly
    chains, of yore
By weapon-smith wrought cunningly, and crested with
    the boar,
That it thereafter never brand nor battle-sword should
    bite.
Nor now at need was Hrunting least of all the helps
    of might
Which Hrothgar's speechman lent to him, the goodly
    hilted blade—
None better among treasures old—the sword of iron
    made,
With twigs of bitter poison steeped, in battle-blood
    annealed,
Never it failed the hand of him who durst it rightly
    wield,
And who dared tread the path of dread, the strong-
    hold of the foe!

                * See Note L.

Not the first time it wrought high deeds. Surely he did not know—
The son of Ecglaf* great in might—what in wine's merriment
He spake, when he that weapon good to better swordsman lent;
For he himself 'neath troubled waves ne'er dared to risk his life
Or work great deeds; and thus he lost the glory of the strife.
Not so the other when he was for battle full arrayed.
"Remember now, great Halfdene's son!" 'twas thus Beowulf said,
"Wise chieftain! kindly lord of men! now for this work I'm dight,
What erst we spake: That if I lose my life to do thee right,
To me when dead in father's stead thou evermore wouldst be.
Guard well my thanes, my comrades true, if battle taketh me.†
And eke the gifts that thou hast given, dear Hrothgar! let them go
To Higelac, that by the gold the lord of Goths may know—
And Hrethel's son, when on the wealth he looks, may see—that I
Have found a bounteous lord of rings, and honour ere I die!

  * Hunferd.   † See Note S.

Let Hunferd famed the heirloom have, the sharp sword wondrous wrought;
With Hrunting will I glory work, or else to death be brought."
 These words he spoke—the lord of Goths—and answer none would bide,
But hastened bold away and plunged within the whelming tide.
 The live-long day he might have sought the ground, but she who there
Haunted the waves for fifty years, bloodthirsty, soon was ware,
Greedy and grim, that from above a man was searching out
The monster's home. At him she sprang and clasped him round about
In fiendish grip; yet not thereby the body could she harm
Shielded with mail, the woven links withstood her loathly arm.
To bottom when the mere-wolf came she dragged into her cave—
Powerless his weapons then to grasp although his heart was brave—
The lord of rings, and in the deep the tusks of sea-beasts tore
The linkèd mail, and uncouth things and monsters vexed him sore.
But now he saw the dreadful hall; there could no water-wight

Nor deadly clasp of waves him touch beneath the roof.
A light
Of fire he saw, a glittering beam, and by its shining
clear
Beheld the she-wolf of the pit, the woman of the
mere!
Fiercely he struck with his war-blade, a stroke so firm
and strong
That on her head the sword rang forth a terrible war-
song.
But now the warrior found the flame of battle * would
not bite,
Nor hurt the life; the blade betrayed its wielder in the
fight.
Full many had it tholed before of combats hand to
hand,
And doomed war-mail and helmet clov'n, but now the
noble brand
For the first time its fame forewent. Yet still Beowulf
stood
Mindful of all his glorious deeds, undaunted, firm of
mood.
In wrath the warrior cast away the chased sword richly
wrought;
(Stiff and steel-edged on earth it lay;) with all his
might he sought
To try the grip of his strong hand. So he who thinks
in strife
To win a deathless fame must do, nor ever care for life!

* 'Battle-flame,' *i.e.* sword.

Reckless of peril then the warrior Goth the shoulders
   grasped
Of Grendel's dam, and full of wrath, in deadly wrestle
   clasped
And flung her on the ground. But him with fierce
   clutch soon she gripped
And paid him back; and overworn, though strong,
   the warrior slipped,
And fell to earth. On him she sat and drew her glaive
   from sheath,
Brown-edged * and broad, athirst to take revenge for
   her son's death.
But on his breast the linked mail lay that point and
   edge withstood,
And saved his life, for then had died the Gothic
   warrior good,
The son of Ecgtheow, 'neath the deep, but that the
   war-mail hard,
The battle-corselet, gave him help; and holy God,
   heaven's guard,
The Lord all-wise, gave judgment true when on his
   feet once more
Beowulf stood. A glorious sword he saw amid the
   store,
An Eoten brand,† the warrior's pride, keen edged, the
   choicest made;
Only it greater was than any weaker man had swayed
In war-play; good and lordly wrought, the giant work
   of old.

* See Note M.   † See Note N.

He seized it by the belted hilt, the Scyldings'
    champion bold!
Hopeless of life, but stern and grim, the mighty blade
    he drew;
Full at her neck he fiercely smote—a stroke so hard
    and true
The bone-rings broke—through flesh foredoomed
    sheer went the sword, and dead
Down on the floor she fell; the chief had joy of work
    well sped!
Gory the glaive, but inner light forth from the blade
    flashed sheen
Even like as in the firmament heaven's candle shines
    serene.
The thane of Higelac then cast his eyes around the
    hall;
And resolute and full of wrath he turned along the wall.
Hard by the hilt he grasped his sword—*that* blade
    had failed him not—
Thirsting to wreak on Grendel now the many evils
    wrought
Not once but oft on Western Danes; when taken in
    their sleep
Were Hrothgar's hearth-companions slain; of them in
    slumber deep
Fifteen devoured, and carried off fifteen—a loathly
    prey.
But now to him the warrior good could well the debt
    repay
When, lying on the bench, he saw war-weary Grendel
    dead

Of wounds at Heorot given. One mighty stroke
    smote off his head;
Far sprang the corse when after death it felt that
    swinging blow.
  The trusty men who there with Hrothgar watched
    the mere below,
Soon saw that all the troubled wave was thick and
    stained with gore;
And grey-haired men together spoke, they weened
    that nevermore
A conqueror the prince would come to see their lord
    again,
Too sure it seemed to most that him the water-wolf
    had slain.
  Now came the noon of day.* The valiant Scyld-
    ings left the shore;
The prince betook him home. But still the strangers
    sat, heart-sore,
Stared at the mere, and hopeless waited, wistful for
    their lord.
Meanwhile with gory drops of war, with battle-sweat,
    the sword
Began to wane away. It melted—wonder 'twas to see—
Like ice when He who time and tide doth rule, true
    God is He,
Looseth the bands of frost, and setteth free the
    fettered wave.
No treasure took the Lord of Goths of all within the
    cave

  * More accurately 'the ninth hour,' *i.e.* about three o'clock.

(Though much he saw) save Grendel's head and
    sword-hilt gold inlaid;
Already melted was the steel, and burnt the naked blade,
So poisonous-hot the blood of that foul sprite who
    there had died.
Soon was he swimming, he who erst fierce battle-
    shock did bide,
And upwards clove the waves. With steady strokes
    then came to land
The seamen's chief, right glad of that great burthen in
    his hand,
His water-spoil.
        The troop of thanes sprang forth to
    greet their lord,
Joyful, and thanking God for him all safe to them
    restored;
And from the warrior speedily were helm and hauberk
    loosed.
    Beneath the clouds the waves grew dark with
    battle-blood transfused,
[But seas and all wide lands were cleansed when that
    bad sprite was dead,
His loan of life at end.] *
        Then glad of heart they turned to tread
With measured step the well-known path; and valiant
    warriors bore
(A heavy task for all their strength) the head from
    the lake-shore.†

    * I have ventured to transpose this passage, which in the original, *ll.* 1620–1622, interrupts the hero's swim ashore.
    † See Note O.

THE RETURN FROM THE BATTLE.

Scarce Grendel's head could four men bear upon
    the battle-spear;
But soon the fourteen glorious Goths to the gold-hall
    drew near,
And proudly in the midst of them their lord trod o'er
    the mead.
Then, honour-crowned, the chief of thanes, the man of
    daring deed,
The warrior fierce in fight, to greet king Hrothgar
    came once more;
And by the hair was borne the head of Grendel on the
    floor—
Where men were wont to drink—before the queen
    and every knight—
A ghastly thing, and all men gazed upon that
    wondrous sight.
Then spake Beowulf, Ecgtheow's son: "Lo!-
    joyfully we bring—
Lord of the Scyldings! Halfdene's son! that thou
    may'st see the thing—
Token of glory, this wave-spoil! I hardly saved my
    life—
Hardly 'neath waters urged the war; lost was by
    rights the strife

Unless that God had shielded me. Albeit weapon good
With Hrunting could I nought achieve; but for my helper stood
Man's Ruler, and upon the wall before me I could see
A great sword hanging, (oftentimes the hopeless guideth He!)
So that the weapon I could draw. In fight then did I kill
The keepers of the house—such hap was mine; but that war-bill—
The naked blade—was all burnt up, when hottest battle-gore
And blood outsprang. Yet from the foes away the hilt I bore,
And as was meet avenged the wrongs and death-throes of the Danes.
Now may'st thou sleep, I promise thee, amid thy band of thanes,
Thy people's warriors—knights and youths—careless in Heorot here.
No death of earl, O Scyldings lord! from that side need'st thou fear
As once thou didst!"

The golden hilt, by giants wrought of yore,
Was given into the prince's hand—the aged warrior hoar.
When devils fell the lord of Danes that wondrous smith-work took.

When with his mother God's grim foe, hell-doomed, the world forsook,
Into his hands it passed, on earth the best of kings was he,
Of those who dealt in Scanian lands treasures by either sea.

  On the old hilt did Hrothgar gaze; thereon was graven true
How rose the strife of old, when flood and streaming waters slew
The giant race puffed up with pride. (A folk estranged were they
From God eternal; their reward th' Almighty did repay
In whelming waves at last.) And on the guard-plate's shining gold
In Runic staves was marked aright, and full set forth, and told
For whom that sword of iron choice, and hilt with knotted snake
Had first been wrought.

  Silent were all; then Halfdene's wise son spake:
"Lo! now may he who true and right among the folk will stand,
Who all the past remembers well—old warder of the land—
Now may he say that born to rule this earl must surely be!
Around wide ways, o'er every folk Beowulf, friend to me!

Thy glory high is raised. Thou keepest it with
    modest mood,
Thy might with wisdom. Now will I my love to
    thee make good
As erst we spoke together. Thou shalt be for many
    a day
A comfort to thy people, thou shalt be thy warriors'
    stay !
To noble Scyldings, Ecgwel's heirs, not so was
    Heremod,
Nor for their pleasure grew he up, but for a fatal
    load
And deadly bane to Danish folk; in wrathful mood
    he slew
His board-mates and his comrades, till he all alone
    withdrew,
Great though he was, from joys of men. Though
    with the bliss of might,
And strength, great God exalted him, and high in all
    men's sight
Did set him, yet bloodthirsty waxed the breast-hoard
    in his heart.
Rings gave he never to the Danes as meet it was;
    apart
From joys he dwelt; and therefore met long-lasting
    overthrow—
War's bitter fruit. Now, warned by him, do thou
    true greatness know!
Wise with the lore that comes of years I've told this
    tale to thee.

Great wonder 'tis to tell how God Almighty giveth free,
With boundless love, earldoms and land and wisdom to mankind.
He ruleth all! The high-born man He letteth sometimes find
His heart's desire in large domains, and in the fatherland
The soil beloved and·stronghold bright He giveth to his hand;
And so on earth with kingdom wide and power doth him endow,
That, in the folly of his heart, no end he cares to know.
Happy he lives; disease and eld to him come never near;
No bitter grief may vex his mind, nor foe e'er cause him fear,
But all the world is at his will; he nothing knows of wrong,
Till overweening pride within him grows and waxes strong,
When sleeps the watchman of the soul—a sleep beset with woe!
Close is the slayer dread whose bolt flies deadly from the bow;
The shaft through all his armour shot, stands grievous in his breast.
At that strange summons of the fiend still finds his sin no rest;

All kept so long still seems too small; his heart is
 full of greed;
For valour's prize he deals no ring; forgets or will not
 heed
The coming fate, for glory's Lord hath ever round
 him cast
Full measure of all earthly bliss. And so it haps at
 last
Death-doomed the shattered body lies; the realm
 another takes
Who freely deals the gifts of earls, and whom no
 terrors shakes.
O dear Beowulf, best of men! of that fell crime
 beware!
Choose the eternal, better rede; for pride take thou
 no care,
Great warrior! Now a little while thy fortune shineth
 bright—
Eftsoons shall sickness or the sword asunder part thy
 might,
Or licking fire, or whelming flood, mace-blow, or
 arrow's flight,
Or dire old age, or flash of eye, stop thee and hide
 the light;
And soon shalt thou, O lord of men! in death o'er-
 whelmèd lie!
Thus o'er the Ring-Danes fifty years I ruled
 beneath the sky,
And guarded them from many a tribe all o'er this
 middle-earth

With spear and sword, until no foe had I round heaven's girth.
Lo! then on me and on my land came change,—joy turned to woe,
When Grendel, man's old enemy, became my deadly foe;
And for that bane sore grief of heart I've borne continually.
Yet thanks be to eternal God that still the light I see,
And fix my eyes—old troubles past—on yonder gory head!
  Now sit thee down, thou famed in war! Let banquet joys be spread,
And wealth of gifts when morning dawns shall pass between us two!"
  Glad was the Goth at heart, and soon he to his seat withdrew
As Hrothgar bade. Then as before fair was the banquet dight
For valiant men who sat in hall. Dark lowered the helm of night
Upon the band. The nobles rose; the grey-haired Scylding old
Would seek his bed; sore longed for rest the Gothic warrior bold.
To him—toil-weary, travelled far—the hall-thane showed the way,
Who to the sailors of the sea his service day by day,
In every want that they could have, with seemly rev'rence gave.

High rose the house, all golden wrought, where laid
    him down the brave :
There slept the guest until the swarthy raven, blithe
    of heart,
Foretold the coming light, heav'n's joy, when shadows
    all depart.

III.

THE PARTING OF BEOWULF AND HROTHGAR.

The knights made haste, for journey boune, to see
    their folk once more;
The valiant guest would seek again his keel far at the
    shore.
He bade them Hrunting bring, and bade the son of
    Ecglaf take
His sword, the goodly steel; and thanked him for the
    loan; and spake
No word of blame of that edged blade, but said that
    good in fight
And trusty friend he counted it; for he was courteous
    knight.
  Now when on journey boune to go were warriors
    armed complete,
Then went the chief beloved of Danes where on the
    lofty seat

GRENDEL'S MOTHER.

Sat Hrothgar, hero old in war, and greeting thus spake he—
Beowulf, Ecgtheow's son:—"We now, the rovers of the sea
Come from afar, to Higelac again desire to go.
Here nobly didst thou welcome us, and mickle kindness show.
If, for thy greater love, I can on earth in any way
Do war-deeds more than I have done, here am I ready aye!
If tidings come beyond the sea that neighbours make thee fear,
As those who hate thee somewhile did, then for thy help and cheer
A thousand fighting men I'll bring! For Higelac I know,
The lord of Goths, (though young he be, the people's ruler) so
With word and deed will urge me on right well to honour thee,
And bear the spear-shaft to thine aid, if thou in need shouldst be
Of men to help thy strength. And if the king's son Hrethic e'er
In the Goth's halls shall plead to him, friends many he'll find there;
Far countries best are sought by him who is himself the best!"

"The Lord All-knowing," Hrothgar said, "has put within thy breast

These ordered words. More seemly speech from
    youth I never heard—
Strong is thy might, thy spirit just, and wise thy spoken
    word !
And well I ween if so it be that Hrethel's heir, thy lord,
The people's guard, shall die by spear, or battle's
    cruel sword,
Or steel, or sickness, while thou liv'st, the Sea-Goths
    could not choose
A better king for treasure-ward, if thou wilt not refuse
The kingship of thy folk. Belovèd Beowulf! more
    and more
Thy spirit pleaseth me! The strifes and bitter
    thoughts of yore
Between Gar-Danes and Gothic men thy deeds have
    laid to sleep,
And peace between them aye shall be while I this
    wide realm keep ;
Their treasures common be, and each shall speak the
    other fair ;
Across the sea, the gannets' bath, the ring-stemmed
    ships shall bear
Gifts and love-tokens ; every way unblamed the folk I
    know
As in old wise, close knit shall be alike to friend and
    foe."
    Then Halfdene's son, the shield of earls, twelve
        gifts gave to his hand,
And bade him with these treasures seek his people
    dear and land,

In happiness and soon come back. And then the
    high-born king,
The Scyldings' lord, the good knight, kissed, and
    round his neck did cling;
He wept aloud—the grey-haired man; yet now in
    eld's decay
Of two things looked for most he hoped that they in
    after day
With joy might meet again in hall. So for the man
    he yearned
These heart-throes could he not forbear; but deep
    the longing burned
Within his heart for him beloved—in bonds of
    thought held tight.
  Then glad of gifts, of treasure proud, Beowulf the
    good knight
Trod o'er the grassy mead. The ship at anchor still
    abode
The coming of her lord. And oft was praised upon
    the road
The gift of Hrothgar; blameless king was he in every
    way
Till robbed of glory's joy by eld that many doth
    affray.

IV.

THE RETURN OF BEOWULF TO HIS OWN LAND.

Then came the band of valiant youths together to the shore;
All clad in mail and corselets linked. The warder as before
Was watchful of the earl's return; but not with words of pride
From sea-cliff greeted he the guests; to meet them did he ride,
And said that freely to the ship the knights of Wederland
In corselets sheen might go. The ring-stemmed bark upon the strand
Sea-worthy loaded they with steeds, and gifts, and battle-gear;
And over Hrothgar's hoarded wealth did high the mast uprear.
Beowulf to the boat-ward gave a sword all wrought with gold,
So that on mead-bench afterwards that gift and heirloom old
Made him more honoured be. On board the ship then did he leap

And pushed off from the Danish land to plough the waters deep.
Firm to the mast was lashed the sail; the vessel groaned aloud;
Winds hindered not her course o'er seas to that wave-floater proud;
With foamy throat and wreathèd stem the traveller of the main
O'er billows sped, and surging flood, till they could see again
The Gothic cliffs and well-known shore. The keel upon the land
Drave up, wind-thrust, and took the ground. Soon ready at the strand
The warder of the harbour stood, who had for many a day
Waited the dear men's coming back, far looking o'er the bay.
The ship, wide-bosomed, fast he made with anchor on the beach,
That never raging breakers' might the goodly craft should reach;
And bade them land the nobles' wealth, the gems and beaten gold,
Not far from thence where they might seek the treasure-giver's hold.
   There Higelac the son of Hrethel, near the water wall,
Dwelt with his thanes at home; in goodly house and lofty hall

A mighty king; with Hygd for wife, well nurtured,
    wise, though young;
Not many winters had she dwelt the palace bowers
    among,
Yet Hæreth's daughter was not mean, nor e'er to
    Gothic folk
Niggard of gifts and precious things.
                       (Foul was the sin that woke
In Thrytho's heart—the haughty queen. Never com-
    panion sweet—
None save her lord alone so bold—her eyes dared full
    to meet;
But him she doomed to bonds of death, his hands in
    fetters laid,
And straightway then the sword was grasped, deep
    bit the deadly blade,
And baleful slaughter was revealed! A deed un-
    womanly,
For woman e'er to do, though fair beyond compare
    she be—
Weaver of peace—with groundless wrath a husband
    dear to slay!
Rightly for that the son of Heming drove her far
    away.
    Yet o'er their ale men said less ill and people's-woe
        she wrought
When, through the wisdom of her sire, by valiant Offa
    sought,
High-born and decked with gold she went across the
    yellow seas,

And there, enthroned in Offa's hall, henceforth she spent at ease
Her days of life in wedded love with that great warrior-king;
The happiest he, of all mankind, as I have heard them sing,
By both the seas, upon the earth; wide-famed through every land;
Sharp was his spear in battle-shock, and free his open hand!
With wisdom did he hold his realm till for the warrior's stay
Rose Garmund's nephew, Heming's son, Eomær the bold in fray.) *

O'er sands and sea-paths and wide shore now had Beowulf gone
With all his men. Forth from the south the sun, earth's candle, shone.
Proudly they went until they heard that, young and brave, the king,
Ongentheow's slayer, shield of earls, in burg dealt gift and ring.
Beowulf's coming speedily was told to Higelac—
That living still and safe from fight, his shield-mate had come back—
The warrior's shelter—to the town, and now to court drew near.
Swift for the guests, as bade the chief, the hall did they make clear;

* See Note P.

And, kinsman facing kinsman, sat the victor in the fight
Before the king, who with great words, in set speech ordered right,
Greeted his friend beloved.
With drinks of mead around the hall
Went Hæreth's child; she loved the folk; and to the proud ones all
She gave the cup.
Then Higelac, with eager thirst to hear
All the adventures of the Goths, began his comrade dear
To question fair in lofty hall: "How sped ye on the way,
Beowulf loved! when suddenly thou thought'st to seek the fray,
And war in Heort o'er salt seas far? Couldst thou do anything
To heal the griefs, too widely known, of Hrothgar the great king?
For that I suffered pain and woe,—I trusted not the feat
For thee, dear friend! I long besought that thou wouldst nowise meet
That deadly fiend, but let the Danes themselves with Grendel fight.
Thanks be to God that safe and sound I have thee in my sight!"

"Lord Higelac!" Beowulf said, "well known to many a man

The mighty clash, and time of strife, that in the place
    began
'Twixt me and Grendel, there where he had many
    sorrows brought
And death among the Scyldings proud. Vengeance
    for that I wrought,
And none of Grendel's kin on earth need boast that
    darkling strife,
Long as the loathly race may keep, in fens beset, their
    life.
  First to the hall of men I went, king Hrothgar
    there to greet;
And straightway Halfdene's mighty son appointed me
    a seat
Beside his son whene'er he knew the purpose of my
    mind.
It was a joyous company; I never yet did find
In all my life, 'neath heaven's vault, 'mong guests
    more merriment.
All round the floor to greet the youths the good queen
    sometimes went,
And often ere she took her seat to one she gave a ring;
And sometimes to the earls and knights the daughter
    of the king
(Fraware her name, I heard them say) in order ale-cups
    bare,
And treasures bright to heroes dealt. Young, decked
    with gold, and fair,
Betrothed to Froda's happy son; for so has he de-
    creed—

The ruler of the Scyldings' realm—and profit counts
    indeed
That with this wife the feuds and strife may all be
    laid to rest.
Yet death's spear droops but for a while, though bride
    be of the best,
After a people's overthrow! And much may it
    displease
The ruler of the Hathobards,* and every thane who
    sees
Some Danish knight attend the bride, 'mong courtiers,
    on the floor,
Vain of the sword with belted hilt that men of old
    time wore,—
The treasure of the Hathobards while they that
    weapon kept,—
Till to unequal shield-play were their loved com-
    panions swept,
And their own lives. Then at the feast may one who
    sees the glaive—
Some spearman old, remembering all the slaughter of
    the brave—
In bitter mood and grief begin with counsel dark to
    spur
The youthful warrior's soul to rage, and battle-woes
    upstir,

---

* 'Hathobards.' Grein thinks these are the Lombards, or Langobardi. They, as well as their king Ingeld—'Froda's happy son'—are mentioned in the 'Traveller's Tale.' See the passage quoted in Note K.

And thus will say: 'Seest thou my chief! that sword, the dear-loved blade
Thy father bore in his last fight, in helmet stern arrayed,
What time the Danes, the Scyldings fierce, slew him and kept the field,
And retribution there was none when death the heroes sealed?
Now here the son of one of those who slew him treads the hall—
Vain of the spoil, of slaughter proud—bearing the treasures all
That thou shouldst rightly have!'
                    With biting words and hinted crime
At every turn he eggs him on, until there comes a time
When, for his father's deeds death-doomed, the lady's thane shall sleep
Blood-stained beneath the stroke of sword; and all the oaths, sworn deep
By earls, on both sides broken be; fierce war shall Ingeld hold
Thenceforth, and in its waves of grief shall love of wife grow cold!
Friendship and love of Hathobards, I therefore count not sure;
And 'twixt them and the Danes the peace will scarce methinks endure.
    But now of Grendel will I speak, that thou mayst fully know,
O treasure-giver! how at last the heroes fight did go.

Soon as heav'n's gem o'er earth had glided came the wrathful sprite,
Eve's servant dread, to search for us who kept the hall aright.
On Hondscio fiercely then he fell—on him who foremost lay,
A belted warrior doomed to die—and Grendel's mouth did slay
Our valiant thane, and swallowed up the loved man's body all.
But not with empty hands to go forth from the gilded hall,
Intent on ill, and bloody toothed, the murderer, proud of strength,
With grasping hand next felt for me. His glove of wondrous length
Hung down, with cunning bands made fast, and craftily o'erwrought
With devils' might and dragon skins; and fierce the monster sought
To slay me, guiltless, as he'd slain full many a man before.
Not so could he when in my wrath upright I stood once more!
  Too long it were to tell how I did to that people's-bane
Mete vengeance due for all his sins; with deeds did I maintain
The honour of thy folk, my chief! He broke away and fled,

And tasted joy of life a while; yet there his right
   hand dread
Remained behind for sign in Heort; and thence in
   doleful mood
He sought the bottom of the mere.
                              The Scyldings' ruler good,
Next day when we sat down to feast, with gifts and
   beaten gold
Gave me reward for that death-close. There song
   and tale were told.
The agèd Scylding, asking much, would tell of days
   gone by;
Or warrior sometimes bid the harp in strains of joy
   reply,
Or wake a true and tender lay; sometimes again the
   king,
Wide-hearted, would in fitting place recount some
   wondrous thing;
Or yet again an agèd knight, eld-bound, would some-
   times tell
The youths of doughty deeds in war, making his heart
   swell,
Wise with the lore of many years, rememb'ring all the
   past.
   And thus we there the livelong day took pleasure,
      till at last
The next night came to men. Then Grendel's
   mother, fiercely bent
On swift revenge for all her griefs, her woful journey
   went.

Dead was her son, the Weder's foe! A knight she boldly slew,
The monstrous 'hag, t' avenge her child; and there, the wise and true,
Lay Æschere passed away from life! Nor when the morning came
Might Danish people burn him there, death-weary, in the flame,
Nor dear one lay on bale of fire; for in her grasp she bore
The corse beneath the mountain flood. Was never grief so sore
Of all that Hrothgar long had tholed. Then prayed he by thy life,
The sorrowing chief, that I some feat would do 'neath waters' strife,
Some daring deed of earlship there; and promised me reward.
    Wide-known it is how then I sought the grim and grisly guard
Of that abyss of waves. Awhile we struggled hand to hand—
The waters bubbling with hot gore—and with my mighty brand
From Grendel's dam I smote the head down in that hidden hall.
Hardly from thence I bore my life—as yet not doomed to fall—
And many gifts the shield of earls, the son of Half-dene gave.

For seemly lived that people's-king ; the proud meed
    of the brave
I nowise missed in that reward, for, all to honour me,
Treasures the son of Halfdene gave, which I would
    bring to thee
O warrior king! to deck thee well! From thee all
    favours flow,
And saving thee, O Higelac! no kinsman chief I
    know."
  Then bade he bring the boar-head crest, the war-
    helm towering proud,
The battle-mail and war-sword good; and set speech
    uttered loud:
"Me Hrothgar gave this battle-gear; and all its
    history
The wise king straitly bade me tell: 'King Heregar,
    said he,
'The lord of Scyldings had it long, but not for that
    would yield
The breast-weed sooner to his son—the valiant in the
    field,
His Hereward, though dearly loved.' Do thou enjoy
    it well!"
  And close behind these treasures came, as I have
    heard folk tell,
Four steeds alike of dapple grey; and steeds and
    treasures too
Beowulf gave to Higelac. So should a kinsman do,
And nowise for another weave with hidden craft a
    snare,

Or plot a comrade's death. To Higelac right loving
    care
His nephew showed, and kindly things each for the
    other thought.
    To Hygd, I heard, Beowulf gave the treasure
    wondrous wrought,
The necklace that Queen Waltheow gave—a monarch's
    daughter she!
Three steeds withal, all goodly shaped, and saddled
    fair to see.
Well was her breast adorned, I ween, when she that
    necklace wore!
    Thus Ecgtheow's son with kindly deeds himself
    right nobly bore,
A man well known in battle-strife, a follower after
    right;
He smote no hearth-mates in their drink; and though
    the greatest might
Of men was his—with glorious gifts him so did God
    adorn—
The bold in war was mild of heart. Long was he held
    in scorn,
Worthless the Goth-men counted him; nor would the
    warriors lord
Much honour ever give to him when seated at the
    board;
For many a time they said that slack was he, and
    sluggish knight;
But to the glorious man at last all wrong was turned
    to right.

[LINE 2191–2207.] GRENDEL'S MOTHER.

Then bade the king, the bold in war, the shield of
 earls, bring in
The sword of Hrethel dight with gold; 'mong all the
 Gothic kin
No better treasure was there then of every kind of
 sword.
He laid it in Beowulf's lap, and gave him seat as lord,
And house withal, and thousands sev'n.
 That realm was native land
To each of them; but right to rule fell to the stronger
 hand
Of Higelac,—the better man obtained that kingdom
 wide.
Changed was it all in later days and war's o'erwhelming
 tide,
When Higelac was killed, and 'neath the shield-wall
 Hardred lay
Slain by the sword, when Scylfings bold, the warriors
 fierce in fray,
Sought him with their victorious host, and did to
 death in fight
The sister's son of Hereric.

DIARY OF
AMMONIUS.

PART III.

THE FIRE DRAKE.

THE ARGUMENT.

Beowulf, having succeeded to the kingdom of the Weder-Goths, had ruled the folk gloriously for fifty years, when the fiery dragon began to lay waste the land. With twelve companions Beowulf goes to do battle with the dragon. He tells the story of his life, and bids his men farewell. Then, with the help of Wiglaf, he kills the dragon, but is wounded to the death, and dies after Wiglaf has brought to him part of the hoard from the dragon's cave. Wiglaf denounces the dastards who shrank from helping their lord. He sends a message home, and bids preparation be made to burn Beowulf's body, which is laid on the pyre and consumed amid the wailing and tears of his sorrowing people.

I.

HOW THE DRAGON GOT THE HOARD AND WASTED THE LAND.

Then afterwards the kingdom wide passed to Beowulf's hand.
He ruled it well for fifty years, old guardian of the land,
And prudent king, till in dark nights began the dragon's sway
Who in the high cliff kept the hoard, upon the moorland grey;
Unknown to men the path below. . . .*

* * * * * *

Great heaps of treasure of old time in that earth-cavern lay,

---

* In the MS. the next sixteen lines are in such a ruinous condition that even with the help of the ingenious conjectures of Kemble, Thorpe, and Grein, it is well-nigh impossible to make sense of them. I do not therefore attempt to translate them. As well as can be made out we are told that a certain thrall, flying from the displeasure of his lord, found the dragon asleep by the hoard, and took away a cup as a peace offering to his master. The dragon awaking missed the cup, and in revenge wasted the land with fire.

The heritage of noble men, which he of olden day,
I wot not who, with anxious care had hidden,—treasures good.
Ere then had death swept all away, and sad was he of mood
Who longest tarried there alone,—the last of valiant men.
Delay he sought that yet awhile he might enjoy again
His treasure. Ready stood the hill, made strong by subtle lore,
Upon the plain, below the ness, hard by the billowy shore.
In it the guardian of the rings that lordly treasure laid,
A heavy load of plated gold, and dark the spell he said:
"O earth! keep thou the warriors' hoard which men may keep no more!
Lo! upon thee by valiant men 'twas gained in days of yore.
But war and death have swept away my comrades every one;
Of those who saw the joys of hall to wield the sword there's none,
Or fill the beaker goodly wrought. Gone are the brave elsewhere!
From frowning helmet dight with gold must fall the plating fair;
They sleep who would have kept it bright! The mail that bite of sword
O'er clashing shield in fight withstood must follow its dead lord.

Never again shall corselet ring as help the warriors bear
To comrades far! No joy of harp, no sound of music there!
Around the hall no good hawk flies, in court no coursers tread!
Before the baleful stroke of death all shapes of life are fled!"
　Thus mournfully he told his grief, and day and night he wept,
Left lonely there till waves of death his sad heart over-swept.
　The goodly hoard was open found by that old darkling foe
Who dwelleth flaming in the hills,—the dragon bringing woe—
Who roams by night begirt with fire, by land-folk far beheld.
There in the cavern shall he dwell to many winters eld,
And guard therein the heathen gold—no whit the better he!
　Three hundred years beneath the earth the people's enemy
With mighty strength his hoard-house kept, till angered by the thrall
Who took the chased cup to his lord to make his peace withal.
Then was the treasure robbed, the hoard of rings was borne away,

And granted was the poor man's bene. Men's work of olden day
For the first time the lord beheld. But when the dragon woke
Was wrath renewed; the fierce of heart scented along the rock,
And found the footprints of the foe; for near the dragon's head
With stealthy craft his steps had gone. (Thus safe may he be led
From woes and pains whom God's grace keeps, as yet undoomed to die.)
Closely the hoard-ward searched the ground, the man to find thereby
Who while he slept had done him wrong, and hotly raging chased
Around the hill, but found him not in all the heathy waste.
Yet eager for the bloody strife, back to the cave he turned
To see his hoard, and quickly found a man the way had learned
To that great wealth of gold. Then hardly would the hoard-ward stay—
So wrath was he—till evening came, athirst that men should pay
Dear for his drinking-cup with fire; and when the day was spent,
Ev'n to his wish, no more in den would he abide, but went,

With flames engirdled, blazing forth.
                              Like as beginning dread
To land-folk—soon the bitter end fell on their leader's head!
  Then spued the fiend out flames of fire and burned the dwellings fair;
Baneful to men the lightnings flashed; the hate that winged the air
Willed death to every living thing. Wide was his bitter wrath
And slaughter seen; and far and near that scather of the Goth
Wronged them with hatred—brought them low—and then ere break of day
Betook him to his hoard again in secret hall that lay.
The land-folk had he girt with fire and burning brand and bale,
Trusting his stronghold and his might; him nought did they avail!
Then to Beowulf sooth and swift the dreadful tidings came
That his fair hall, gift-seat* of Goths, was burnt in waves of flame.
This worst of griefs his kindly heart with bitter sorrow tore;
The wise king weened that God eternal he had angered sore

* *Gif stól.* The place where gifts and rewards, the 'rings,' of which we hear so much, were given.

By sin against the old command; and in his breast awoke
Dark thoughts that were not wont with him. The stronghold of the folk,
The isle beyond, and all the land, the fiery drake had burned.
The Weder chief, the warrior king, his mind to vengeance turned.
A wondrous shield the lord of earls bade make of iron good,
For well he knew that 'gainst the flames no help was linden wood.
The end of life's lent days on earth the good prince must abide,
And with him too the worm, though long the hoard had he enjoyed.
The ring-bestower scorned to seek with host and great array
The wide-winged dragon; never yet did battle him affray,
And nothing recked he of his foe his valour and his might.
For many a hair-breadth 'scape in war, and many a stress of fight
Had he outlived, since Hrothgar's hall, victorious, he made clean,
Grappling with Grendel's loathy race. (Nor least was that, I ween,
Of battle-grips when Higelac, the people's dear loved lord,

THE FIRE DRAKE.

The heir of Hrethel, king of Goths, struck down by battle-sword,
In Friesland slain in clash of fight, lay weltering in his blood.
By his own might Beowulf 'scaped, for he could stem the flood;
And when he plunged into the sea his single arm upbore
The battle-weed of thirty men.* Their war on foot no more
Might Hetwars boast who there had stood before him shield in hand;†
Few from the dauntless warrior 'scaped to see their native land!
Then o'er the seals-path swam forlorn Beowulf, all alone,
Back to his folk, where realm, and hoard, and rings, and kingly throne
Were offered him by Hygd. Her child—now Higelac was dead—
She trusted not to keep the land from foreign foemen dread.
Yet nowise could they, desolate, with him prevail the more
The realm to rule as Hardred's lord; rather with friendly lore

---

* This refers, I think, to the 'strength of thirty men' which Beowulf's arm is said to bear. See p. 19, l. 379.

† Omne robur in pedite (Tacitus, Ger. 30). Quoted with reference to this passage by Grimm (Gesch. d. Deutschen Sprache, ii. 591).

In honour ever 'mong the folk he nobly Hardred kept,
Till older grown he ruled the Goths.
                               O'er seas in exile swept
To him the sons of Ohthere fled.* Rebellion they had made
'Gainst the great lord, the best sea-king of all who treasure swayed
In Swedish realms, the Scylfings' chief. But thence came Hardred's woe;
For there the son of Higelac was struck a deadly blow
At banquet by the swing of sword; and then, when he lay cold,
The son of Ongentheow went home, and let Beowulf hold
The kingly throne and rule the Goths. Good king in truth was he!
  In later days for this defeat he sought revenged to be,
To hapless Eadgils proved a friend, and sailing with his folk,
O'er wide seas Ohthere's son upheld with war and weapon stroke,
Revenged his woful fortunes cold and reft the king of life.†
  Thus mighty deeds had Ecgtheow's son outlived, and every strife,
And venture perilous, till come was that one fatal day
When with the dragon he must fight.
                               Then did he take his way,

---

* See Note Q.   † 'The King'—Onela.

The lord of Goths, to seek the drake—he and eleven more
With wrathful hearts. He learned the place whence sprang the trouble sore
And warriors' woe, for in his lap the goodly cup was laid
By him who knew, and who the band thirteen in number made.
Beginner of the strife was he, but poor he was of soul,
And humbly did he show the way, unwilling, to the hole
He only knew—beneath the earth, hard by the billowy sea
And troubled waves—a cavern full of wires* and jewelry.
The monster guard, the fighter fierce, of old below the ground
His gold-hoard kept—not easily by man could it be found.

* 'Wires' for twisting into brooches, bracelets, and the like.

BEOWULF'S SPEECH.

The Goths' gold-friend, the warrior-king, sat down
    upon the ness,
And to his hearth-mates bade farewell. His heart was
    in distress,
Death-bound and wavering; Weird was come im-
    measurably near
To seek the treasure of his soul, meet the old man,
    and shear
sunder life and body; flesh should not for long array
The prince's soul.* And thus Beowulf, Ecgtheow's
    son, did say :
"Many the times of strife I've seen in youth, and
    battle dire.
I mind it all! Seven winters old was I when from
    my sire
The lord of wealth, the peoples chief, took me and
    brought me up;
Mindful of kin king Hrethel gave me fee and food
    and cup;
A knight in burg, as dear to him as his own children
    were,

    * Poor soul, the centre of my sinful earth,
      Fool'd by these rebel powers that thee array.
                  Shakespear. Sonnet cxlvi.

Her'bald or Hæthcyn or my Higelac.
>By chance unfair
A brother's deed the bed of death did for the firstborn
 strew,
When Hæthcyn's bolt from bended bow his dear loved
 kinsman slew;
He missed the mark and shot his friend; and with a
 bloody dart
Brother did brother slay;—foul sin; a lasting grief of
 heart;—
A death unpriced;*—and unavenged the prince's life
 must be.
 Then sadly as an old carle bides while on the gallows
  tree
His young son rides; and maketh wail, and song
 with sorrow fraught,
When, joy of ravens, hangs his son, and he himself can
 nought,
Sore stricken now in years, to help. For ever comes
 to mind
Each morning that his heir is dead; he careth not to find
Another in the burg to keep the heritage when one
Fate-driven has met his death. Then on the dwelling
 of his son
He gazes sorrowful of heart, the guest-hall lying waste,
The wind-swept ruins silent now; in grave are sleeping
 fast
Warrior and knight; the melody of harp is heard no
 more;

   * See Note R.

No merriment is in the courts as once in days of yore!
Then to his bed he turneth him, and chaunteth lay on lay
Of sorrow; all too wide to him seem grange and meadow-way.
 Ev'n so for Herebald heart-grief the Weder's shelter dreed;
Upon his slayer not a whit could he make good the deed,
Nor hate him for the hateful deed although he could not love.
Thus gave he o'er the joy of men, so sore did grief him move;
God's light he chose,* and left his heirs, as wealthy men must do,
The land and city of the folk when life no more he knew.
 Then between Swedes and Goths was guilt and strife o'er waters wide,
And fighting fierce and mutual hate as soon as Hrethel died;
And while the sons of Ongentheow were bold in war and strong
Peace would they none beyond the seas, but slaughter grim, and wrong
They ofttimes wrought round Hrosnaburg. Revenge for crime and strife,—
Well known it is—my kinsman took—bought dear with Hæthcyn's life,

   * See Note S.

For slaughtered lay the lord of Goths. But when the morrow broke
His brother's fall a brother's hand avenged with weapon stroke.
Then Ongentheow met Eofor—there his war-helm cloven fell,
And death-pale lay the Scylfing old; the hand remembered well
The feud, and shrank not from the blow.
       Then for the gifts he gave
Right well I paid my Higelac in war with flashing glaive;
He gave me land and pleasant home. For him there was no need
To seek 'mong Gifthas,* or Gar-Danes, or in the realm of Swede,
To buy with bounties meaner knights! Ever alone in front
So would I go before his host, and so would bear the brunt
Through all my life, while lasts this sword that aye has served me well
Since erst Dæghrefen by my hand—the Hugas' † champion—fell

---

* 'Gifthas' have been identified with the Gepidæ.

† 'Hugas' identified with the Chauci of Tacitus. This Huga champion was probably the slayer of Higelac, and would, according to custom, have despoiled him of his ornaments. See p. 55, where the necklace is mentioned. Frisians and Chauci, according to Grimm (Deutsche Sprache, 677 n.), are different names for the same people.

In sight of men; and never might he bring the
    bosom's pride—
The necklace—to the Frisian king; the standard-
    bearer died,
In valour noble, on the field—but not with sword-
    stroke killed,
Only in deadly wrestle grasped his beating heart I
    stilled,
And crushed the body lay! But now must hand and
    edge of sword—
And now must keenly tempered blade do battle for
    the hoard!"

III.

THE FIGHT WITH THE DRAGON.

Beowulf spoke his last proud words: "In youth
    I much have warred,
And still for battle will I seek,—my people's faithful
    guard,—
And work great deeds if on me comes the monster
    from his den.'
Then took the helmet-bearer bold farewell of all his
    men,
His comrades dear, and said: "No sword or weapon
    would I bear

Against the worm, if else I wist how I might grasp him fair,
As Grendel long ago I did. But now I ween will break
Hot flame and poisonous breath on me, and therefore do I take
My shield and arms; the mountain's guard one inch I would not flee.
Between us at the cliff as Weird shall mete so let it be!
My heart is fixed; no other boast I'll make o'er that winged foe.
Bide ye upon the hillside here, my mail-clad men, to know,
In corselet safe, which of us two shall, after battle hot,
Have hap to overlive his wounds. For you this task is not;
'Tis all unmeet for any man, save me alone, to try
My strength 'gainst fiends and challenge sway. By force of arms will I
The treasure win, or else in fight let swift death take your lord!"

 Beside his shield, 'neath helmet stern, he rose and took his sword—
The warrior proud—below the cliff, trusting his single might.
No coward's feat was that! Then he, who many a clash of fight,
And battle fierce when armies meet—the bravest of the brave—

Had overlived, saw by the rock where from an arching cave
A stream gushed from the mountain side, with hot flames all aglow,
So that unhurt by dragon's fire no man might pass below
Down to the hoard. Forth from his breast, in wrath, he sent a shout;
The strong heart stormed; that battle-cry resounded round about;
Beneath the hoar-grey stone it went, and stirred up deadly hate;
The hoard-ward knew the voice of man; for peace 'twas now too late.
  Then from the rock the monster's breath like burning reek did blow;
Earth bellowed; and the lord of Goths to meet the grisly foe
His shield edge thrust. The coiled worm's heart was stirred for strife to crave.
Already had the warrior-king unsheathed his keen old glaive,
(Dreadful to each his deadly foe!) and mail-clad, firm of mood,
While swift the dragon coiled himself, behind his high shield stood.
And from his coils the fiery drake to doom wild-rushing came!
  Less while the shield his life and body sheltered from the flame

Than he had hoped—the mighty lord—in that first time and tide
When he could wield it. Not for him did Weird the battle guide."
He raised his hand—with his good sword he smote the dread of hue
So that on bone the edge gave way—the brown blade bit less true
Than sore beset its lord had need. Yet at the awful stroke
Wroth grew the mountain's guard; death-fire he cast, and wide outbroke
The scathing flames. No victory the friend of Goths had won;
The naked war-bill failed at need—so should it ne'er have done,
That best of steel! For Ecgtheow's son no easy lot was there—
To leave the earth and find a home at dragon's will elsewhere.
Thus men must leave this fleeting life!
       But soon together pressed
These foes again. The treasure's guard, emboldened, swelled his breast
Anew with poisonous breath; and he who long had ruled the land
Tholed grievous straits, girt round with flame; beside him stood no band
Of comrades true, the ætheling's sons, of valour proved in strife—

For crouched low in the wood they lay each one to save his life!
  Yet one man's heart with sorrow swelled,—for he who feels aright
Can kindred ne'er forget,—the son of Wohstan, Wiglaf hight,
Shield-warrior bold, the Scylfings' chief; he saw his good lord bear
'Neath battle-helm the flames, and thought of all his gifts whilere,
Rich Wægmund lands, and folk-rights all which once his sire did wield;
No more could he forbear; he grasped his yellow linden shield,
Drew the old sword that Eanmund, Ohthere's son, 'mong men had left—
(Him Wohstan in the battle slew, outcast, of friends bereft; *
And to his kinsman took his mail, brown helm, and eoten-glaive.
Then Onela to him his comrade's arms and war-gear gave;
And, though his brother's son was slain, spake never word of feud.
Long years the corselet Wohstan kept, the sword and treasure good,
Till mighty deeds his son could do as did his sires of old.

  * The history of Wiglaf's sword which comes in so awkwardly here is a part of the confused narrative of events which I have endeavoured to make clear in Note Q.

When full of years from life he fared, much battle-gear
    untold
He gave to Wiglaf 'mong the Goths. Now by his
    liege lord fought
For the first time the warrior-youth, yet his heart
    melted not,
Nor in the battle failed him then his father's last
    bequest,
As speedily the dragon found when they together
    pressed)—
And Wiglaf then, with sorrowing heart, thus to his
    comrades spake
With measured words : "I mind the time that we did
    promise make
To our good lord who gave us rings, in beer-hall, o'er
    the mead,
For this war-gear, keen sword and helm, to pay in
    such-like need,
When for this task from all his host he chose us at
    his will,
And stirred us up to glorious deeds; and gave me
    treasures still,
Because he held us spearmen good, and helmet-
    bearers true.
  And though our lord, the people's ruler, thought
    alone to do
His mighty work,—for more than men has he in
    daring deed
And glory wrought,—yet now is come the day that he
    hath need

Of valiant warriors' strength. To help our chief then let us go
Though fierce the flaming terror burns! For me I'd liefer so,
God wot, that with my lord's the fire should clasp my body too!
Unseemly 'tis, methinks, that we—unless the foe we slew,
And saved the Weder-prince's life—should bear our shields away.
Full well I wot, not his desert that he alone to-day
Of all the noble Goths should thole these straits, and fall in fight!
We'll share with him the sword and helm, corselet and buckler bright!"
  Then rushing through the deadly reek with shield his lord to aid,
Few were his words: "O dear Beowulf! thou in youth hast said
That never in thy life wouldst thou let fame from thee depart;
O by the glory thou hast won, thou ætheling firm of heart!
Now with thy might strike for thy life! Here stand I by thy side."
  Scarce had he spoken when the fiend, malignant, flaming wide,
The dragon came in wrath to seek his hated foe again.
Burned the broad targe in waves of fire; no help was corselet then,

To that brave youth; he shelter took beneath his kinsman's shield—
His own was burnt away. Then did the king his war-bill wield,
Mindful of fame, and on the head he dealt a mighty stroke.
But that good sword, the old grey steel—Nægling—gave way and broke!—
Not to Beowulf was it given that steel should lend him aid
In battle-strife; too strong the arm whose swing o'ertasked the blade.
Though wondrous keen the sword he bore for him it nought did gain.
 A third time then the fiery drake, the people's direful bane,
Bent on revenge, when room was given, rushed on the warrior bold,
Burning and fierce, and clasped his neck in many a deadly fold,
So that the king was drenched with gore, in streams the life-blood flowed.
Then, at his liege lord's need, the earl undying valour showed,
And inborn strength and worth. His head he heeded not to save,
Burnt was his valiant hand as help with all his strength he gave.
Yet somewhat did the warrior armed beat down the deadly foe,

Plunged deep the goodly hilted sword, and made the flames burn low.
Back to the king his senses came; the fatal dirk he drew,
Which on his corselet hung full sharp, and stabbed the dragon through.

IV.

THE DEATH OF BEOWULF.

The noble kinsmen felled the foe; their valour took his life,
And laid him low. Like them always be knight and thane in strife!
Last of the prince's victories it was, in life's-work got
By his own deeds!
 The wound that erst the dragon gave grew hot,
And swelled; and soon Beowulf felt death-throes within his breast,
And inward poison working. Then deep-pondering he pressed
Close to the rock and sat him down. On giant-work he gazed
And saw how there the arch of stone, firm on its pillars raised,
Held in the everlasting cave.
 Then Wiglaf water bore

And with his hands bathed tenderly his dear lord drenched in gore,
And with the battle all forspent, and did his helm undo.
Then of his wound Beowulf spoke—that gash of deathly hue—
Full well he knew his day of life, his joy of earth was done,
His death exceeding near at hand, his tale of days outrun—
And thus he said: "Now to my son my battle-weed I'd give
If of my body any heir to guard it yet did live.
For fifty years I've ruled the folk. Of all the peoples near
No king durst meet me with his hosts nor cause me aught to fear.
At home I bode my time; held well my own; no quarrels sought;
Nor swore an oath unrighteously. With death-wounds now o'er-wrought
In that I may rejoice! When life and body sundered be
No kinsman's slaughter can the Lord of man impute to me!
  Now quickly go, dear Wiglaf! Seek the hoard beneath grey stone,
Now that the dragon lies asleep, with grievous wounds o'erthrown,
Of goods bereft; and use all speed that I may close behold.

The jewels cunning wrought, old wealth, and all the store of gold,
And so when treasure rich is mine that I may pass away
More easily from life and land I've held this many a day!"
  Then at the words, as I have heard, straightway did Wohstan's heir
Obey his wounded dying lord; his linked war-coat he bare,
And ring-mail 'neath the cavern's roof. And when he passed the seat
The brave thane, proud of victory, saw lying at his feet
Much jewel-work and glittering gold, and wonders on the wall—
The dragon's den, where stood the old night-flyer's beakers all,
The cups of bygone men—unbrightened—shorn of ornament;
And many a rusty helmet old, and many armlets bent
And closed with cunning skill.
                The gold that lay within the den,
Keep it who will, might well surpass all treasures known to men.
  And high above the hoard he saw a golden banner stand,
Fastened with cunning finger-craft, most wondrous work of hand;
And from it flashed a beam of light that he could see the ground,

And search for all the precious things. No dragon there he found,
Slain by the sword was he.
                      And thus by one man, I've been told,
The hoard within the hill was robbed—the giant-work of old.
Dishes and cups into his lap he piled as he thought right;
The banner too he took away—the shining beacon bright—
And brass-shod sword with iron blade which that old leader wore,
Who long while kept these treasures all, and fiery terrors bore
Fierce-welling, hot before the hoard at midnight, till he died.
   Wealth-laden now the messenger him swiftly backward hied,
His brave heart torn with doubts if he alive should find again
The Weder's lord where he had left him fainting on the plain.
His treasures bearing forth, he found, near death, and drenched in gore,
The mighty chief. With water then he sprinkled him once more,
Till through the treas'ry of the heart the word's point forced its way,
And sadly gazing on the wealth thus did the old man say:

"Now to the King of glory, Lord Eternal, Lord of all,
I utter thanks for these fair things on which my eyes
  do fall;
And for my folk that I could win thus much before
  my death.
Wisely I've bought this treasured hoard at price of
  my last breath!
  Fulfil ye all the people's need! Here may I be no
    more.
Bid my brave warriors build for me upon the lofty shore
After the bale-fire, a bright mound, which, high on
  Hronésness,
Shall keep my folk in mind of me; and sailors all
  who press
Their long-ships o'er the misty deep shall henceforth
  call it aye
Beowulf's Mound!"
        The fearless-hearted prince now put away
The golden ring from off his neck; his helmet
  wrought with gold,
And ring, and corselet then he gave to his young
  spearman bold;
Bade him enjoy them well, and said: "Alone thou'rt
  left, the last
Of all our Wægmund race; my kinsmen, earls of
  might, have passed,
Weird-driv'n, to doom; and thither too I go."
        Of his heart's thought
Twas the last word the old man spake ere he the
  bale-fire sought,—

The hotly raging waves of flame; and from its dwell-
  ing fared
His spirit forth to seek the doom for righteous men
  prepared.

V

WIGLAF AND THE DASTARDS.

'Twas hard for youth untried to see his much-loved
  leader dead,
Stretched pale and livid on the ground. Yet there
  the Scather dread,
By wounds subdued, bereft of life, the monstrous
  earth-drake lay.
No longer might the coilèd worm his treasured ring-
  hoard sway,
Killed by the iron sword,—the hammer's work * most
  sharp and bright—
And near his hoard-house, on the earth, grovelled the
  wide-of-flight
Wound-quieted; careering now through midnight air
  no more
In sport, and proudly making show of all his treasures'
  store,

---

* *Homera láf*, the 'leavings,' the result, of the hammer in forging. So l. 1032, the sword is called *féla láf*, 'the file's work.'

But by the warriors' handiwork down-fallen to the ground!
  Surely on earth few men have thriv'n, however daring found
In every deed—men holding power—for all that I have heard,
Who 'gainst a poison-scather's breath rushed on, or ever stirred
A ring-hall with their hands, if they its warden found awake—
The dweller in the mound. In death did now Beowulf take
His share of lordly treasure. Each found end of fleeting life!
  Stole from the holt soon afterwards the laggards in the strife,
The weak and faithless (ten they were), who in their lord's sore need
Had never dared to brandish spear. Now shields and battle-weed
Ashamed they bore where lay their chief, and there on Wiglaf gazed.
  The shoulder of his liege-lord there the weary warrior raised,
With water sought to waken him, but all his toil was vain;
On earth he might not, dearly wished, his leader's life retain,
Nor change th' Almighty's will. God's doom to every man shall rede

According to his works; and so ev'n now He doth indeed.
  Stern was the young man's ready speech to those dishonoured men;
On them, unloved, he sadly looked, and answered them again:
"Lo! he may say, who truth will speak, that he who gave to you
The battle-gear that now ye wear, and gifts—your liege-lord true,
(When on the ale-bench oft he dealt to sitters in the hall
Corselet and helm, as lord to thanes, the costliest of all
That he could find or far or near,) too plainly flung away
Most grievously this battle-weed! When hard bested in fray,
Nowise of comrades in his work the people's king could boast!
Yet God, the Lord of victories, when valour's need was most,
So granted him that all alone his weapon vengeance wrought!
Little the succour I could give,—yet past my power I sought
To help my kinsman; when with sword the deadly foe I smote
Ever the fiercer ran the fire that burned within his throat.

Around their lord in his sore need too few did helpers stand!
Now gifts of treasure and of sword, all joy of home and land,
Shall fail your kin! Of land-rights void each tribesman shall return
When nobles far away your flight and shameful deed shall learn!
Better is death for every earl than life with blasted name!" *

VI.

THE MESSAGE HOME.

Then at the stronghold did he bid the mighty feat proclaim,
On seacliff high, where by their shields the earls in troubled mood
Sat all the livelong day, and looked for evil or for good—
Their loved chief's death or his return! Nor silent then was he
Who brought the tidings to the ness, but told all truthfully:
"On deathbed fast the lord of Goths, kind chief of Weder folk,

* See Note T.

Dwells in death's sleep by dragon slain! And sick with dagger's stroke
Beside him lies his deadly foe; with sword could nought be done
To wound the monster any way. Now Wiglaf, Wohstan's son,
Sits by Beowulf,—earl by earl,—the living by the dead;
By friend and foe with reverence due he keepeth lyke-wake dread!

  Now time of strife the folk may see when our king's death is known
To Franks and Frisians plain; for fierce the feud with Hugas sown
When Higelac with battle-ships invaded Frisian land.
There Hetwars vanquished him in war, and with the stronger hand
The glory won till, 'mid his host, they forced the mail-clad knight
To yield and die. To warriors then nowise the spoil of fight
Their leader gave; and never since have Merwings * kindly been.
Nor yet shall we from Swedish folk have love or truth, I ween;
For wide 'tis known how Ongentheow slew Hæthcyn, Hrethel's heir,
At Ravenswood, when in their pride the Scylfing host whilere

    * 'Merwings'—the Merovingians.

Fell on the Goths; and Ohthere's sire, wise, terrible, and old,
Struck down and slew the great sea-chief; and, though bereft of gold,
Set free again his wedded wife, his bride (the mother she
Of Ohthere and of Onela); and then the enemy
He followed till they hardly reached, lordless, the Raven's wood.
With mighty host he then beset the weary few who stood,
A wounded remnant of the sword; and often through the night
He threatened woe on that poor band, and said ere morning light
Sword-edge should greet them, and that some on gallows-tree should ride
For sport to ravens; but good cheer came with the morning tide
To mournful men, when loud they heard the horn of Higelac—
The trumpet blast—and to his folk the warrior-prince came back!
  Then wide were seen the bloody tracks and strife of Swede and Goth,
And how the peoples—each with each—awakened deadly wrath.
  To seek his fastness grieving much, then went with all his men
The prudent chief: earl Ongentheow drew back to home again.

Of Higelac the proud he heard—his war and battle-
   might—
And weened not to withstand him there, or with the
   Goths to fight,
Or from the bold sea-rovers save his treasure, sons,
   and bride;
And thence the old man turned away the earthen wall
   beside.
 Then was pursuit of Swedes decreed—banner and
   victory
To Higelac! Forth went the Hrethlings* o'er the
   peaceful lea
Till round the stronghold fierce they thronged, and
   with the edge of sword
The grey-haired Ongentheow was slain; for there the
   people's lord
Must yield himself to Eofor's doom! At him so
   smote amain
Wulf, Wonred's son, that at the blow blood burst
   from every vein
Beneath his hair; but not the less the old king un-
   affrayed
Turned on him and for that fell stroke a worse
   exchange repaid;
For before Wonred's nimble son could deal another
   blow
Atwain the helmet on his head the old man cleft, and
   low

* 'Hrethlings,' *i.e.* Goths, the people of Hrethel, the father of Higelac.

On earth fell Wulf all stained with blood; but not yet doomed to die,
With grievous wound he 'scaped.
　　　　　　　　　When there he saw his brother lie
Eofor—brave thane of Higelac—broke down with his broad blade
O'er buckler wall the eoten-helm, and old sword eoten-made;
Down fell the king, the people's guard—his life was shorn away.
　Many they were who bound the wounds of kinsmen on that day,
Quick raising them when room was made, and they the battle-field
Could hold while warrior warrior spoiled. The hilted falchion steeled,
The iron corselet, and the helm, from Ongentheow they tore,
And all the hoary leader's arms to Higelac they bore;
Who took the spoil, and promised fair rewards to all his men;
And kept his word; the lord of Goths, when home he came again,
On Eofor and on Wulf bestowed rich treasures for the fight—
A hundred thousand's worth in land and twisted armlets bright;
(Since they such mighty deeds had done no man on middle-earth
For such rewards could scoff at them); and to adorn the hearth

His only daughter Higelac to Eofor gave to wife.
> Lo! there the cruel hate of men, the enmity and strife!

Therefore I ween that us with war the Swedes will overwhelm,
Whene'er they hear our lord is dead, who kept the hoard and realm
Erewhile 'gainst every foe, when bravely Scylfing heroes fell—
Fulfilled the counsel of the folk, and every way did well.
> Now haste is best that we may look upon the people's king,

And carry to the bale-fire him who gave us many a ring!
Nor shall the goods of any man be with the warrior burned,
For treasure yonder lies untold, and wealth too dearly earned!
Now at the last with his own life he bought these armlets fair
Which fire shall eat and flame o'erlap. No earl shall treasure bear
For mem'ry's sake; nor maiden bright her neck with rings adorn,
But oftentimes, of gold bereft, strange lands shall tread forlorn,
Now that the leader of the host has ceased from joy of song,
And sport and laughter.

Cold at morn shall many a spear ere long
With hands be grasped and brandished high! No
 more the harper's strain
Shall warrior wake; but swarthy ravens, busy o'er the
 slain,
With clamour manifold shall tell the eagles how they
 sped
At their repast, when with the wolves they battened
 on the dead!"

VII.

THE BURNING OF BEOWULF'S BODY.

Thus spoke the warrior bold his hateful news; nor
 greatly lied
In word or weird forecast. Uprose the band, and sadly hied
With streaming tears 'neath Eagle's Ness the wonder
 to behold.
There found they him who gave them rings oft in
 the times of old
Dead on his bier upon the sand; passed was the
 latest breath
Of their good lord; the warrior-king had died a
 wondrous death.
But first they saw a stranger thing—the loathly worm
 lay low

Over against him on the plain. Scorched with the
 burning glow
The fire-drake fifty measured feet lay prone—a horror
 dread—
Who through the night took aëry joys, and downward
 would have fled
Back to his den; now fast in death no more would
 see his cave.
Beaker and bowl beside him stood, and dish, and
 costly glaive,
Rust-eaten like the things in earth a thousand years
 that dwell.
The heritage of men long syne, that gold, with mighty
 spell
Had so been girt about that never man that treasure-
 hall
Had stirred, unless that God Himself, who men
 protecteth all,
True King of victories, had giv'n to whomsoe'er He
 would,
Ev'n to the man whom He thought meet, to ope that
 treasure good.
 Thus was it seen his toil was lost, unrighteously
 who filled
The cave with riches; for though some its keeper erst
 had killed,
Yet vengeance stern was dealt for wrong; and where
 the wonder where
That glorious earl to meet the end of his life's-work
 should fare,

When in mead-hall among his kin he may no longer
    dwell?
Thus to Beowulf happed it then when with dire hate
    he fell
Upon the warden of the hill; to him was all unknown
What thing should sunder him from life; and how, till
    doomsday shone,
The mighty chiefs who hid the hoard had solemnly
    declared
That guilty sinner should he be, by devils fast ensnared,
Fixed in hell-bonds, and stained with crime, whoe'er
    should tread the place.
Yet gold he loved not; rather sought to see his
    grace.
  Then Wiglaf, Wohstan's son, thus spake: "Oft for
    the sake of one
Must many earls dree wretchedness, as we e'en now
    have done!
To our dear lord, the kingdom's guide, no counsel
    could we bear
To shun the keeper of the gold, and let him still lie
    there
Where long he'd lain, and in his den the end of time
    abide.
High destiny have we fulfilled; the hoard is opened
    wide,
And fiercely won! Too strong the fate that drove
    our leader here!
  I went within and saw it all—the dwelling's
    precious gear—

When room was made, and passage giv'n, but not in
   friendly wise,
Below the cliff. With haste I grasped a great and
   heavy prize
Of hoarded wealth, and bore it all out hither to my
   king.
Still did he live, still knew and felt, and sadly many a
   thing
The old man said; and all of you he bade me greet,
   and prayed
For all the deeds of your kind lord that ye should
   cause be made,
Where stood the funeral pile, a great and high and
   glorious mound;
As he was warrior worthiest 'mong men the world
   around,
While burg and treasure still were his.
                              Now let us haste once more
To see the wonders 'neath the rock, and seek the
   precious store!
I'll be your guide, that plenteous gold and rings ye
   close may see.
When out we come again let bier prepared and ready
   be;
And then the man beloved, our lord, forth let us bear
   away
Beneath the shelter of his God, where he must bide
   for aye."
   Then Wohstan's son, the bold in war, for his good
      leader bade

Full many knights (the lords of lands and those who
  vassals swayed)
Bring wood for burning from afar: "For now must
  fire devour,
And wan flames eat, the doughtiest knight e'er bode
  the iron shower,
Ofttimes when o'er the shield-wall sent the storm of
  arrows flew
From bowstring and the feathered shaft the bolt held
  straight and true!"
  Forthwith did Wohstan's wise son call together
  from the band
Sev'n of the king's best thanes, himself the eighth who
  there did stand
Beneath the dreadful roof. A lighted torch the
  warrior bore
Who led the way. No lots they cast what man
  should spoil the store
When much unguarded there they saw in hall that
  idle lay.
And little mournèd any man when out they bore away
With speed the precious treasure forth.*
              The dragon-worm they cast
Down from the cliff and gave the flood to keep, and
  waves hold fast,
The guardian of the hoard. And every kind of
  twisted gold,
Past counting on a wain they laid; and bore the
  warrior old,

* See Note U.

Their prince, to Hronésness.
                        For him the Gothic people dight
Upon the earth a lofty pile, with helm and corselet bright
And war-shield hung, as he besought; and in the midst they laid
Their noble prince, their lord beloved. And then the warriors made
A mighty bale-fire on the mound. The smoke of wood uprushed
Black o'er the blaze and roaring flame; and every wind was hushed;
Was weeping all around; till fire consumed with burning breath
The body. Sorrowful and sad they mourned their liege lord's death.
Such dirge the elf-locked crone gave forth. . . .
    *   *   *   *
The heavens were swallowed up in smoke.
                        A barrow, broad and high,
The Weder folk raised on the cliff, which sailors might descry
Far o'er the sea; and of the brave they built the beacon-mound
In ten days' time; and that great pile did with a wall gird round
As wise men deemed most fit and right. And all the precious things

---

* Here the text is in a very ruinous state—only fragments of words remaining. See Note V.

Brave men had taken from the hoard—the jewels and
 the rings—
They laid upon the mound; and let the gold lie in
 the earth,
And earth the lordly treasure keep, where, still as
 little worth
To men as ever, yet it lies!
      Then nobles twelve—the chief—
The bold in war—around the barrow rode and spoke
 their grief.
They mourned their king, and chanted dirge, and
 much of him they said;
His worthiness they praised, and judged his deeds
 with tender dread;
As well beseemeth it that men their dear lord's praise
 should show,
And love him with their hearts when he from lent
 flesh forth must go.
His hearthmates thus and Gothic folk bewailed
 their prince's fall,
'Mong kings of earth the mildest, kindest, lovingest of
 all!

NOTES.

NOTE A.

THE SEA BURIAL OF SCYLD.

IN the *Times* of 21st June, 1880, an interesting account was given of the discovery of a Viking ship in a sepulchral mound, called the King's Hill (Kongshaug), on the shores of Christiania Fjord, and the description of the vessel throws much light on the arrangement of the stately bier that bore the dead Scyld on his last long voyage. After a minute account of the ship, with its boats, oars, and "loose beams ending in roughly carved dragons' heads, painted in the same colours as the bows and sides of the vessel—to wit, yellow and black," we read: "All along the sides, nearly from stem to stern, and on the outside, extended a row of circular shields, placed like the scales of a fish; nearly a hundred of these are remaining, partly painted in yellow and black, but in many of them the wood has been consumed and only the central iron plate is preserved. . . . It is now clear that they had only an ornamental purpose, being of very thin wood, not thicker than stiff paste-board, and unable to ward off any serious blow from a sword. In the middle of the vessel a large oaken block, solidly fastened to the bottom, has a square hole for the mast. . . . *In this part of the vessel was built the funereal chamber,* formed by strong planks and beams placed obliquely against each other, and covering a room of nearly fifteen feet square. . . . A few human bones, some shreds of a sort of brocade, several fragments of bridles, saddles, and the like in bronze, silver, and lead, and a couple of metal buttons, one of them with a remarkable representation of a cavalier with lowered lance, are all that has been got together from the mass of earth and peat filling the funereal chamber."

" Þat var ríkra manna siðr, konunga eðr jarla várra jafningja, at þeir lágu í hernaði, ok öfluðu sér fjár ok frama, ok skyldi þat fé eigi til arfs telja, né sonr eptir föður taka, heldr skyldi þat fé í haug leggja hjá sjálfum." (It was the custom of great men, kings or jarls like us, to go on raids and get themselves wealth and fame, and that wealth was never counted heritable, nor might the son take it after his father, but it must be laid in the *haug* beside him.)—Vatnsdæla Saga, in Fornsögur. Leipzig, 1860, p. 4.

The greater the treasure placed beside the dead, the better his appearance in the other world; but the goods must be of his own winning or else the free gifts of his dependents. Thus, when making preparations for the obsequies of Beowulf, the messenger bids the people have no fear, for there is plenty without calling on them to help.

" Nor shall the goods of any man be with the warrior burned,
For treasure yonder lies untold," etc.

modern vessel. No authentic drawing of an old English ship exists, nor any description earlier than Ælfred's account of the vessel he built (Chron. 897), which was evidently considered a great achievement in naval architecture; but I suppose there can be no doubt that the English or Geatic keels differed only slightly, if at all, from the ships of the Danes and Norsemen. Of these several examples have been discovered besides that mentioned in Note A. One in particular found at Nydam, on the eastern coast of Sleswick, is probably the exact counterpart of the ships which bore the English invaders to the shores of Britain. A full description of this vessel, with minute and careful drawings of every part, will be found in Engelhardt's 'Denmark in the Early Iron Age,' London, 1866. It was seventy-seven feet in length and ten feet ten inches in breadth. Stem and stern are exactly alike, so that it might be rowed either way. " On both stems . . . there are ornamental grooves, and each of them shows two large holes which, to judge from the marks of wear, must likely have served to pass the ropes through when the boat was to be hauled on shore." Perhaps the most curious thing about this boat is that " the ribs have perforations corresponding to the clamps [on the planks] through which bast ropes were passed tying planks and ribs together. . . . It is possible that a loose connection between the framework and the planking of the boat served to give more elasticity to the sides, and that boats built in this manner went through the surf and great waves easier than those more strongly built" (Engelhardt, p. 31). In fact, both in appearance and construction it seems to have been not unlike the well-known Massoolah boats which brave the formidable surf at Madras. The Nydam vessel seems to have been propelled entirely by oars, fourteen on each side—at least no mast nor any provision for one has been found.

The representations of ships in the Bayeux tapestry,

although quite conventional, are probably as true for the eighth as for the eleventh century. The later ships were no doubt larger, but the style of ornament, with which we are here chiefly concerned, evidently remained much the same. See especially the ship which bears William himself with its high stem crowned with an elaborately carved lion's head; the ornament at the top of the mast illustrating the lines—

"A banner too of gold
High o'er his head they raised aloft;"

and the shields which are ranged along the gunwale, like the hammocks in a man of war, illustrating the passage, "bright shields o'er the bulwarks borne."

NOTE D.

"BOAR-CRESTED HELMETS," AND "MAIL BY SMITH-CRAFT WROUGHT."

At Benty Grange, in Derbyshire, a barrow of the Anglo-Saxon period was opened in 1848, and among the valuable relics found in it was the frame of a helmet, which is thus described by the finder, Mr. Bateman. It "consists of a skeleton formed of iron bands radiating from the crown of the head and riveted to a circle of the same metal which encompassed the brow.* From the impression on the metal it is evident that the outside was covered with plates of horn disposed diagonally, so as to produce a herring-bone pattern. The ends of these plates were secured beneath with strips of horn corresponding with the iron framework, and attached to it by ornamental rivets of silver at intervals of about an inch and a half from each other . . . and on the crown of the helmet is

* This framework, which rises high over the head, may perhaps be the *wala* which (p. 47) I have translated "boss."

an elliptical bronze plate supporting the figure of an animal carved in iron with bronze eyes, now much corroded but perfectly distinct as the representation of a hog" (Bateman's Ten Years' Diggings, quoted in Grave-Mounds and their Contents, by L. Jewitt, p. 252). The accompanying woodcut shows the boar standing on the top of the helmet like the crest of a knight in later days. I have some doubt, however, if this helmet corresponds to those spoken of in the poem. There is in the Banff Museum a helmet of brass *shaped* like a boar's head, which, if I remember rightly, is said to have come from some Norse place of sepulture in Scotland, and it is possible that this rather than the Benty Grange type may be the helmet thus described :—

<pre>
            eofor líc sciónon
     ofer hleór-beran gehroden golde
     fáh and f r-heard ferh wearde heóld.   303-5.
             (Boar shapes shone
       Over cheek-pieces plated with gold
  Many hued and fire hardened the boar kept guard.) *
</pre>

The remains of a coat of mail were also found at Benty Grange. "The iron chain-work . . . consists of a large number of links of two kinds, attached to each other by small rings half an inch in diameter ; one kind are flat and lozenge-shaped, about an inch and a half long ; the others are all of one kind, but of different lengths, varying from four to ten inches. They are simply lengths of square rod iron, with perforated ends through which pass the rings connecting them with the diamond-shaped links ; they all show the impression of cloth over a considerable part of the surface" (Grave-Mounds, p. 254).

* Insigne superstitionis formas aprorum gestant (Tacitus, Ger. 45).

Note E.

THE ARRANGEMENT OF THE HALL.

The following diagram, taken from Dr. Vigfusson's Icelandic Reader, p. 357, shows the arrangement of the hall in Norway, and as we may suppose it to have been at Heorot.

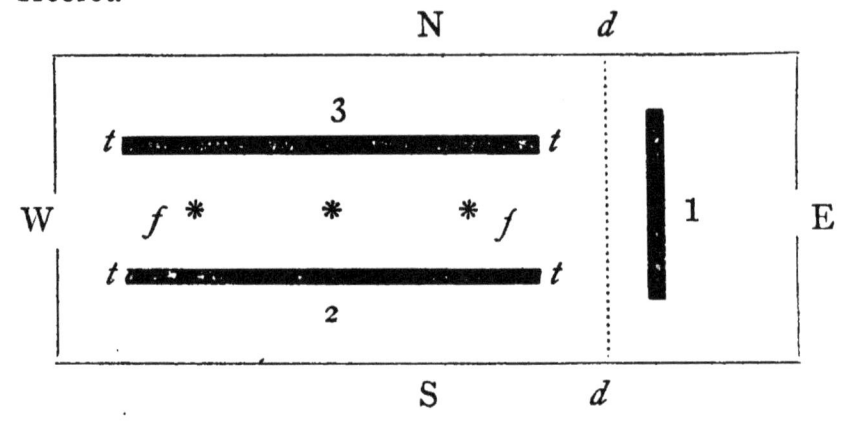

dd, the dais. 1, the dais 'high seat' where the king sat.
2, the high seat. 3, the next distinguished seat.
tt, the tables and benches. These were removable and were cleared away at night when the hall was turned into a sleeping-place.
ff, the fire hearths.
W, the main western entrance; E, a small private entrance.
The queen and the women sat at the cross table on the dais.

Kemble, in a note to the line which says that the Queen sat down beside her lord, observes: "I have all along looked upon this poem as an Angle and not a Saxon work; perhaps these lines may be taken as confirmation of the fact. Among the West Saxons it was not usual for a Queen to sit by her lord upon the throne, and in this feeling the other Saxon tribes must have shared. As late as the eleventh century Æðelwulf gave great offence in Wessex by granting this honour to his wife Judith, a Frankish princess and daughter of Charles the Bald." (Beowulf, vol. ii. App.) Kemble overlooks the fact that it is the Danish custom which the poet here describes, and it seems to have resembled the Norwegian. The Goths, whom Kemble identifies with the Angles, apparently had the more primitive arrangement of the hall in which there was no dais; for in the account of the reception of Beowulf by Higelac the kinsmen are expressly said to face one another—*i.e.* the King on the high seat (2), Beowulf on the next honourable (3), and Queen Hygd is nowhere said to have sat beside her husband.

NOTE F.

"*Thou wilt not need to hide my head.*"

Nó þú mínne þearft hafelan hýdan (445). The exact meaning of this passage is much disputed. Thorpe supposes that it means 'thou wilt have no occasion to bury me, as my body will be devoured by Grendel.' Mr. Arnold takes the same view; so does Grein, though with a note of interrogation; and I confess it seems to me on the whole, though not without difficulties, the most reasonable. But Heyne, in a note to the passage, argues strongly for interpreting it as meaning that Beowulf, having undertaken to do battle with Grendel in the hall, dispenses with the guard of honour, to which otherwise he would have been entitled as a guest of royal birth. This guard in the Anglo-Saxon laws is called *heafod-weard*, 'head guard' (Ger. *haupt wache*), and Heyne quotes Domesday Book I. 252, *quando rex jacebat in hac civitate servabant eum vigilantes XII. honimes de melioribus civitatis*, etc. We may suppose, he adds, that this rule was obligatory on the King himself, when he was visited by a guest of equal rank. It is this guard which is referred to, he thinks, in the passage describing Beowulf's morning visit to Hrothgar after Æschere's slaughter by Grendel's mother (p. 64). See Heyne's Beowulf, p. 90.

Note G.

"Cast up in heaps upon the shore."

This may be a hint of the old fancy that water-beasts go ashore to die. In the story of the Three Caskets in the *Gesta Romanorum* (No. lxvi.) we read: "And when the maid felt that she was in the womb of a whale she smote and made a great fire and grievously wounded the whale with a little knife insomuch that he drew to the land and died; *for that is the kyñde to draw to the land when he shall die.*" (*Gesta Rom.*, Early Eng. Text Soc. Ed., p. 298.)

Note H.

SIGMUND.

In the Norse and the German versions Sigurd, or Sigfried, the son of Sigmund, gets possession of the hoard. The poems of the Edda which contain the Niflung legend may possibly be older than Beowulf, but I think the contrary is more probable, and that we have here the earliest form of the story.

Fitela is the Sinfjötli of the Edda. He was the son of Sigmund, and in the Helgakviða Hundingsbana I. and II., his adventures with his father are obscurely told. In the Sinfjötalok (which, however, is a prose abstract and probably very much later than the poems) he is said to have been killed by poison administered by his stepmother Borghild (Brunhild).

NOTE I.

THE BARD'S TALE.

This story was evidently a popular ballad among the Danes and Goths—so popular indeed that the poet plunges *in medias res* at once and does not stop to tell us how or why the fight began. He little thought that his poem would be read by men so ignorant that they cannot even tell where Finnsburg was, and who know as little of this 'famous victory,' which to him and his hearers seemed so glorious, as old Kaspar did of Blenheim. We can only dimly guess at the sequence of events by piecing together the passage in the text, and the picturesque fragment on the 'Fight at Finnsburg' which Hickes discovered, bound up with a volume of homilies, in the library at Lambeth, and which is printed as an appendix to Beowulf by Kemble, Thorpe, Grein, and Heyne.

Hence, therefore, authorities differ very widely in their interpretation of this obscure story; but, after duly weighing the various explanations of the tale, I read it thus. Finn, the son of Folkwald, was King of the Frisians, and was married to a Danish Princess Hildeburh, the daughter of Hoce. For some unknown reason an attack was made on Finnsburg by a party of Danes under Hnæf (the son of Hoce and the brother of Hildeburh), aided by some Jutes under Hengest. Finn calls his men to arms:

" 'Tis not the daybreak in the east, nor hither dragon flies,
　Nor burn this hall's high pinnacles, but on us foemen rise!
　The grey wolf howls; the ravens cry; the battle-wood clangs loud,
　Shield answering to shaft; the moon shines full beneath the cloud.
　Now to fulfil this people's hate are coming deeds of woe.
　But wake ye now my warriors all! Awake! Your valour show!
　Lift up your hands, fight in the front, and think of glory won!"
　　　　　　　　(*The Fight at Finnsburg*, 3-12.)

The doors of the hall are attacked and defended, and for five days the fight went on, but it is not easy to distinguish the assailants and the assailed. Garulf comes to the door and asks who keeps it, and Sigferd replies:

"'Sigferd my name, the Secga's lord,' quoth he, 'a well-known knight;
Many the troubles I have borne, and many a harder fight,
Yet here whatever thou shalt seek is now decreed for thee!'
Then in the hall was din of strife; broken must buckler be,
And keelèd shield in warrior's hand! Loud rang the castle hall,
Till, foremost of earth's dwellers there, in fight did Garulf fall—
The son of Guthlaf—round him lay the corse of many a foe.
Swarthy and sallow-brown the ravens wandered to and fro;
And brightly flashed the gleaming swords as though all Finnsburg blazed."

(*Ib.* 24-36.)

In the end Hnæf and many of his men were killed, but Finn's loss had also been heavy, and two or more of his sons were among the slain. Finn, therefore, made a peace with Hengest, undertaking to treat the remnant of the Dano-Jutic force as liberally as if they were his own subjects; and it was expressly stipulated that on neither side should any allusion ever be made to the old quarrel, and that any man who did so should be slain with the sword. Then the dead bodies of Hnæf and the sons of Finn were burned on the pile together, Hildeburh weeping sore for her sons and her brother. Some of the Danes seem to have taken service under Finn, and to have been scattered about Friesland; two—Guthlaf and Oslaf—seem to have gone home; but Hengest abode with Finn during the winter, brooding on plans of vengeance. When spring came Hunlafing, whom I take to be Hengest himself, or at any rate a follower of Hengest, killed Finn, and in the confusion which followed the King's death, Hengest and his men sacked the burg and then carried Hildeburh and the spoil back to Denmark.

Grein and Heyne call Hunlafing a man who killed

Hengest, and this interpretation, though I think it adds greatly to the difficulties of the story, is, I admit, the most obvious rendering of the text; but I would, with great diffidence, suggest that *he* in line 1142 (although the immediate antecedent is no doubt Hengest) really means, as the context seem to me clearly to show, not Hengest but Finn.

Mr. Arnold, following the Danish editor Rieger, thinks that Hunlafing was a sword which Finn gave to Hengest as a peace-offering, and he supports this view with many ingenious arguments.

Whether Hengest can be identified with the famous chief who led his Jutes into Kent in 449 is a question which can only be answered doubtfully; but there seems to be no objection to it unless Grein's interpretation be accepted, when of course it is impossible. But if Hengest and Hunlafing are the same person, the Hengest of the poem can hardly be identified with the Hengest of Kent, unless Hunlafing may be taken as a family name (like Scylding, Scylfing, etc.), and not necessarily implying that Hengest was actually the son of Hunlaf.

In the Traveller's Song *Fin Folkwalding* is mentioned as ruler of the Frisian Kin (27); Hnæf is said to rule the Hocings (29); and (31) we find *Sæferð* [*weóld*] *Sycgum*. Evidently this is Sigferd, chief of the Secgas, in the passage quoted above from the 'Fight at Finnsburg.'

Of this and the other episodes Mr. Sweet remarks that "they would be less liable to alteration than those passages which form part of the main narrative, and it is highly probable that among them the oldest parts of the poem are to be found" ('Sketch' already quoted, p. 11). They are in fact samples of the original materials which the poet used in composing the work. We may, however, trace his own hand, I think, in the impossible incident described in l. 1122, of blood gushing from burning corpses, which shows plainly enough that the description

M

was written long after the 'age of burning' had ceased, and that the poet was inventing picturesque touches to heighten the effect of a scene which he could never have personally witnessed.

NOTE K.

HROTHULF.

Hrothulf, the nephew of Hrothgar, was the son of the 'good Halga,' mentioned in the beginning of the poem. He is better known perhaps under the name given him by the Norsemen, Hrolf Kraki. *Kraki*, being interpreted, means a branched stick used as a sort of rude ladder, and there is a pretty story in the Skáldskaparmál of the way in which Hrolf came by this odd nickname. There was a king once in Denmark, it is said, the most famous of the old kings, and the first in gentleness and valour and humility. When he was but a youth there came one day into the hall, where the king was sitting on the high seat, a poor boy who stood before the king and gazed at him. "What do you want, my boy?" said Hrolf. "When I was at home," the boy answered, "I heard it said that King Hrolf at Hleiðr was the greatest man in northern lands, and now here sits on the high seat a little *Kraki*, and they call that the king!" ('A forked stick' would perhaps translate the word best—Hrolf being probably a thin slip of a lad). "Well, my boy," said the king, "you have given me a name, and Hrolf Kraki shall I be called; but it is usual to give something at the name-fastening, and I don't see that you have anything to give that I should care to have, so the gift must be the other way," and with that he took a gold ring from his finger and gave it to the boy.

The 'Traveller' mentions Hrothulf, and says that he

and his uncle Hrothgar very long remained at peace with one another after they crushed the Vikings, defeated Ingeld's army, and beat down the glory of the Heathobards at Heorot. (Traveller's Song, 45-49.) There is something ambiguous in this as well as in the words of our poem, 'there was still peace between them—each faithful to the other,' and Mr. Arnold is perhaps right in thinking that Hrothulf afterwards turned against his uncle.

The passage just quoted from the Traveller's Song is interesting in connection with the political forecast made by Beowulf in his speech to Higelac. (Part II. IV.)

NOTE L.

NICORS.

The Nicor, which here means simply a monstrous water-beast, with perhaps a hint of supernatural malignity in its disposition making it a fitting companion of Grendel and his mother, was in Teutonic mythology a water-goblin taking many shapes, from that of a handsome dapple-grey horse to the half-man half-fish of the merman, or the half-man half-horse of the centaur; and it is evidently a near relation of the kelpies and water-bulls of Scottish superstition. The word, which in various forms is common to all the Teutonic languages, was used by old writers as a translation of 'crocodile' and 'hippopotamus.' It was applied to Odin himself as ruler and soother of the waves. Plants and stones were called after the *nix* or *neck*. A German name for the water-lily is *nixblume;* tufa in Swedish is called *Näcke bròd*, the bread of the water-spirit; and Grimm thinks that the name of the river Neckar may perhaps have some connection with the word. Our 'old Nick' comes from it; and Dr. Vigfusson suggests that *Nep*tunus may be related to Nick. (Icelandic Dict. s. v. *Nykr.*)

In the grey horse shape the nicor could be recognized by its inverted hoofs. If any one ventured to mount on its back it immediately plunged into the water with its prey. Yet it could be captured and made useful for a season ; and Grimm tells a story of an ingenious man at Morland in Bohus—Beowulf's own country—who bridled his nicor so artfully that it could not escape, and ploughed all his fields with it, till by some evil chance the bridle got loose, and the nicor sprang like fire into the sea, dragging the harrow after it. (Deutsche Myth., p. 458.)

Mr. Taylor (Words and Places, p. 223, 3rd ed.) says of the *nikr*, "This dreaded monster, as the Norwegian peasant will gravely assure you, demands every year a human victim, and carries off children who stray too near his abode beneath the waters. In Iceland also Nykr, the water-horse, is still believed to inhabit some of the lonely tarns scattered over the savage region of desolation which occupies the central portion of the island."

The wild creatures foretelling woe to seamen remind us of Scott's—

> "The fishers have heard the water-sprite
> Whose screams forebode that wreck is nigh."

NOTE M.

"BROWN EDGED."

The phrase 'brown edged,' is not a very obvious epithet for a sword, and it would perhaps be better to render *brún* 'grey,' for the word as we now use it appears to have acquired a special signification which did not originally belong to it. It is derived by Grimm (Wörterbuch, s.v. *braun*) from the Gothic *brinnan*, to burn ; and it seems to have meant the colour of things burnt, *i.e.* ashes. Grein's vocabulary shows that with one exception all the applications of the word *brún*, which occurs about a dozen times in Anglo-Saxon poetry, are to swords, weapons, helmets, the sea, waves, and to the Ethiopians. Not one of these, unless the sword or helmet was very rusty indeed, would we now call 'brown.' The exception is in Cynewulf's Phœnix. The poet describes that interesting bird as if he had seen it, and says that its tail is "*brún*, purple, and spotted with black." And brown the Phœnix's tail may be, for anything I know to the contrary.

The Goths planted the word in Italy, but Dante's *l'aer bruno* cannot mean that the evening air was of that reddish hue which we now call brown.

Bishop Percy, in a note to the line in the ballad of Robin Hood and Guy of Gisborne, "with blades both brown and bright," says: "The common epithet for a sword or other offensive weapon in the old metrical romances is *brown*. As 'brown brand,' or 'brown sword,' 'brown bill,' etc., and sometimes even 'bright brown sword.' . . . It would seem from this particularity that our ancestors did not pique themselves upon keeping their weapons bright; perhaps they deemed it more honourable to carry them stained with the blood of their enemies." This seems rather far-fetched. Servile imitation of older poets and the alliterative jingle had probably more to do with the choice of the word as an epithet for a sword than anything else. Dr. Vigfusson's suggestion that the *brown* of the English ballads is the Norse *brugðinn*, 'drawn' (Icel. Dict. s.v. *bregða*) seems to me untenable.

In the 'Fight at Finnsburg,' the raven is called *sealo brún*. 'Sallow brown' in our sense the bird is not, but 'black and sallow-grey' well describes his glossy plumage when the light glances on it.

It might, therefore, have been better to translate the word, here and elsewhere, in the sense in which the Anglo-Saxon poets probably used it—'grey' of any shade from the hue of steel to Ethiopian duskiness.

It may be, however, that *brún* meant simply that the weapon, helmet, etc., had been exposed to the fire—'burnt.' At any rate, we must not suppose that the edge of the sword was brown in our sense of the word.

Heyne renders *brún* 'brown or rather copper red,' and says that the word is applied to a sword 'because it is bronze.' But this explanation seems inadmissible. The swords in Beowulf are always iron, and a poet of the seventh or eighth century had probably never heard of such a thing as a bronze sword.

Note N.

EOTEN.

Eoten is the Anglo-Saxon form of the Norse *iötunn*, and it is, I think, a proof of the Northern origin of the Beowulf legend that this essentially Norse word is peculiar to this poem and, as Grein's vocabulary shows, is found nowhere else in Anglo-Saxon poetry. There is no exact English equivalent for it. If we translate it simply 'giant' we lose, as it seems to me, something of its superhuman significance, for the Jötuns of Scandinavian mythology—the old demigods only half subdued by the later deities—were not mere big men. Their knowledge is more than once spoken of in the songs of the older poetic Edda; the mysteries of the world were called by the Norsemen *jötna rúnar*, 'the runes or secrets of the jötuns;' and the well-known stories of the later prose Edda which tell of Thor's adventures in Jötunheim show clearly that it was not in wisdom, at any rate, that the divine race of Odin surpassed the rude gods of nature.

Hence such phrases as 'eoten sword,' 'eoten helm,' and the like mean not merely that the sword or helmet was very big, but also that it derived some mysterious virtue from its first makers—the possessors of a wisdom now lost to the world for evermore.

No trace of the word exists, I believe, in English popular superstition or phraseology,* but in Scotland, where the northern influence was so much more potent, we meet with it frequently. 'The red Etin,' a monster of cannibal propensities with three heads, is—or rather was, for he is now forgotten—the Scottish counterpart of the giant slain by Jack the Giant-killer; and a hungry man was proverbially said 'to roar for his meat like a reid Etin.' That the story of this monster was once very popular is proved by Sir David Lyndsay's words to James V.:

> "And oft times have I feinyet mony a fable
> . . . . . .
> Of the Reid Etin and the Gyre Carling
> Confortand the when that I saw thee sorry."
> (*The Dreme. Epistil to the King's Grace.*)

as well as by the passage in 'The Complaynt of Scotland,' in which among the tales told by the shepherds is mentioned "the taiyl of the reyde eyttin witht the thre heydis" (Edition of the E. E. Text Soc., p. 63). The story itself is given in Chambers's 'Popular Rhymes of Scotland,' and although it comes from a somewhat dubious source—" Mr. Buchan's curious manuscript collection "—I see no reason to doubt its authenticity. This

---

* Beaumont and Fletcher have it once: "They say the king of Portugal cannot sit at his meat but the giants and the *etins* will come and snatch it from him" ('Knight of the Burning Pestle,' Act i.). As the speaker is an ignorant, foolish woman, it may be perhaps that the word was still occasionally used at that time among the lower classes.

red Etin is evidently the giant in the ballad 'Young Ronald' who

> had three heads upon ae hause [neck]
> Three heads on ae breast bane.

The ballad 'Hynde* Etin' tells of a lady who was captured by this dweller in the woods and bore six children to him, but though the name shows that the legend is old the ballad itself seems to me comparatively modern.

The 'Eldridge Knight' of the ballad of 'Sir Cauline' in Percy's collection is perhaps a later form of the Eoten, and the five-headed giant whom the hero kills is certainly an exaggeration of the terrible Red Etin.

In Sir Tristrem (Fytte i. lxxxvii.) 'Moraunt the noble Knight' is said to have been accounted an 'eten' in battle.

The story of the 'gyre carline,' which was known to Sir David Lyndsay, has been irrecoverably lost, but, as Sir Thomas Browne says of the song the sirens sang, we 'might hazard a wide solution' that she is a later form of Grendel's mother. 'Gyre' Jamieson derives from "Isl. *Geira*, the name of one of the fates,"—rather it should be one of the Vælkyries, the maiden 'choosers of the slain,' who was called *Geirahöð*.

The word *ent* 'giant' (no doubt nearly allied to *eoten*) occurs eight times in Anglo-Saxon poetry (thrice in Beowulf) always in the gen. pl. *enta* and associated with *geweorc*, 'the giant's work.' At p. 126, l. 2717, Beowulf at the mouth of the dragon's cave *seah on enta geweorc*, 'gazed on giants' work.' This seems to have been a stereotyped phrase—like 'Cyclopean walls'—for any structure, natural or artificial, supposed to be too great for the powers of man, and the idea long survived. In

---

* 'Hynde' means gentle. This was a very 'delicate monster' with only one head apparently, and he was no cannibal.

the Scottish version of the Romance of Sir Tristrem we read :—

> "Tristrem with Hodain [his favourite dog]
> A wilde best he sleugh ;
> In on *erthe house* thai layn,
> Ther hadde thai iole y-nough ;
> *Etenes bi old dayn*
> *Had wrought it* with outen wough."
> (*Sir Tristrem: Fytte* iii. xvii.)

And so, too, we have 'Devil's dykes,' 'Devil's punchbowls,' 'Giant's causeways,' etc.

There is probably no real connection between the great volcano of Sicily, whose name is said to come from a Phœnician word meaning 'furnace' and the eotens of the north, but it is at least curious that the abode of the Cyclops, who in many respects, and especially as expert blacksmiths, closely resemble the eotens, should be called Mount *Ætna*, the mountain, as we might translate it, 'of the eotens.' (See Grimm's remarks on the connection between Wayland and Hephæstus in D. M., p. 351.)

The passage at p. 52, describing the graven work on the sword-hilt, refers to the biblical giants who are called *giganta cyn*, not eotens.

NOTE O.

GRENDEL.

This word is found in various forms in most of the Teutonic languages, and generally with some connoted diabolical or infernal significance. It means bolt or bar, and is associated in this sense with the 'bolts of hell.' But it also means simply beam, Mod. Ger. *grindel*, whence probably Grindelwald. Mr. Arnold says : "Perhaps a simpler etymology may be found in the O.E. adj.

gryndel, 'wrathful.' See *Sir Gawayne and the Green Knight*, published by the E. Eng. Text Society. . . . Gervase of Tilbury (whose date is about 1200) has a chapter 'De Grant et Incendiis.' Grant is a spirit in the form of a horse with flaming eyes, who appears in public places to warn people of coming fires. Liebrecht connects *Grant* with *Grendel* and also with *Granta*, the old name of the river Cam." (Beowulf, p. 214.)

Dr. Haigh finds traces of the fiend not only "in Grindlesmere in Wiltshire and Grindelespytt in Worcestershire, to which the late Mr. Kemble thought that some association with traditions like the story in question had given origin; but in that of Grindleton in Yorkshire, and Crindale dykes on the Roman wall. Near to the latter there is Grindon lough and Grandy's knowe; and in the neighbourhood of Hart there is a parish named Grindon, and Grandy's close, all apparently having the name of the same person—once no doubt a powerful chieftain settled in the county of Durham; and singularly enough in the close proximity to Grandy's close there is Thrum's law, *i.e.* the 'giant's hill.'" (Haigh's Anglo-Saxon Sagas, p. 24.)

While stories of fiery dragons are common enough in all countries, and have all a certain family likeness, it is curious that no trace of the Grendel legend should have been found anywhere except perhaps a faint solitary echo of it far away in Iceland. Dr. Vigfusson has pointed out[*] that some features of the story may be detected in the Grettis Saga, now accessible to English readers in the fine translation of Messrs. Magnusson and Morris.

There is first Grettir's struggle with the fiend Glámr (chap. xxxv.). The hero watches for the monster who nightly haunted the house, and the fight takes place partly in the hall, partly outside, just as in Beowulf's encounter with Grendel. The furniture and fittings of the house

---

[*] Sturlunga Saga. Oxford, 1878. Prolegomena, p. xlix.

are wrecked in the struggle, but Glámr is killed.* Secondly (ch. lxv.), Grettir, long after the Glámr adventure and in a totally different place, watches for the nightly visit of a 'troll-wife,' and as before there is a desperate conflict in the hall, but Grettir is carried off, and it is only when they come to the gulf of the river that he can get his sword loose, *strike off her arm*, and throw her down the torrent. Thirdly (ch. lxvi.), in continuation of this adventure, Grettir dives into a cave below a waterfall and finds there a dreadful giant, whom he kills. The priest who accompanied the hero, and was watching at the edge of the abyss, goes home when he sees the blood swirling down the stream, thinking that Grettir had been slain, just as Hrothgar and his men departed, thinking Beowulf was killed, when they saw the water of the mere all suffused with blood.

There can be no doubt, I think, that we have here some features of the Beowulf-Grendel story, but altered and rearranged, as might be expected seeing that the two versions are separated by an interval of five hundred years.

There may be perhaps some vague reminiscence of the story in the ballad of Sir Cauline in Bishop Percy's collection (Hale's and Furnivall's Ed., vol. iii.). The hero fights with the 'Eldridge Knight,'† and overcomes him *by striking off his hand*, which he bears, along with '*the Eldridge sword as hard as any flint*,' to his lady-love,

---

* The conclusion of this passage, where Glámr lays the curse of his eyes on Grettir, is very fine. "They have Glám's eyes," the Icelandic saying is, "who see things other than they are." Thence the Scotch 'glamour.'

† 'Eldridge' means 'wild,' 'hideous,' 'unearthly.' Gawain Douglas translates *Ætnæos fratres* (Æneid iii. 678) 'they elriche brethir.' The witches pursue Tam o' Shanter ' wi' mony an eldritch screech and hollo.' Sir W. Scott certainly got from Sir Cauline the hint for the host's tale of King Malcolm and the Elfin Knight in the third canto of Marmion.

the King's daughter, *as tokens of his victory*. A similar incident occurs in the Romance of Sir Tristrem. The hero tears off the hand of the giant Urgan and bears it away. (Scott's edition, Fytte iii. iv.)

Grendel is more than once said to dwell or walk alone. Giants were supposed to love solitude—like Polyphemus they 'dwelt apart in lawlessness of mind.' In the Gnomic verses (Grein, ii. 347) it is said:

> Þyrs sceal on fenne gewunian ána innan lande.
> (The giant shall dwell in the fen alone in the land.)

With the description of Grendel devouring Beowulf's comrade, compare the account of Polyphemus eating up the companions of Ulysses in the ninth book of the Odyssey.

Von Moltke, writing of the plague in Bulgaria in 1837, says that one day they met a miserable creature to whom they gave alms, and on asking what ailed her she replied: "The woman who wanders by night and sets her mark on people has taken away my husband and children. I am left alone." (Briefe über zustände in der Turkei 1835-39, p. 158.) This curious personification of the plague might be Grendel's mother.

NOTE P.

THRYTHO.

Grein remarks that just as the poet (in Part I. IV.), after speaking of the deeds and the fame of the Wælsing Sigmund, passes suddenly to Heremod whose inglorious end sits the glory of Sigmund and of Beowulf in a clearer light, so here the ferocity of Thrytho seems to be told to enhance the gentleness of Hygd.

He then quotes from the history of the Two Offas,

ascribed (erroneously, Mr. Luard says *) to Matthew Paris, the story of the second Offa's marriage to Drida, a Frankish princess, and cousin of Charlemagne. She was a woman of wonderful beauty, but of a very evil disposition, and had been condemned to death for a most flagitious crime—the precise nature of which is not mentioned. But as by reason of her royal birth she might not be delivered to fire or sword, she was sent adrift upon the sea in an unmanned boat scantily provided with the necessaries of life. After long tossing about she was thrown, hunger-stricken and wretched, on the coast of King Offa's country. Being brought before the king, she told him that the cause of her misery was the cruelty of a low-born man, whose offer of marriage she had rejected as beneath her station. The king, moved by her misfortunes, her charms, and her graceful speech, gave her to his mother's care, and in a few days, having recovered from the effects of her perilous voyage, and now again shining in all the splendour of her beauty, she seemed the fairest woman that had ever been seen. But with her beauty reappeared also the ferocity of her disposition, and she repaid the loving care of her benefactress with haughty and insulting words—'after the fashion of her country,' as the biographer adds. The king, who knew nothing of this, paid a visit to his guest, and was so struck with her wonderful beauty that he fell violently in love with her and married her, to the great grief of his parents. Her subsequent wickedness is set forth at large in the history, but I need not further pursue the story.

It is evident that the author of the lives of the Two Offas had heard of the legend told in Beowulf, and misled by the identity of name—for by a marvellous coincidence the wife of the historical Offa of Mercia, if Matthew Paris

* Matt. Paris, Chronica Majora (Rolls series), vol. I. pref. p. xxxii., note.

is to be trusted, seems really to have been called Drida—*
he transferred to this king's reign a tale which properly
belongs to the first Offa, son of Garmund (the Offa of
Beowulf), who is said to have ruled over the Angles in
the fourth century.

According to their biographer the matrimonial ventures
of both the Offas were somewhat hazardous. Offa I.
while out hunting met a beautiful lady, who told him
that she was the daughter of a regulus of York, and that
she had been driven forth and exposed to the perils of the
wilderness because she would not yield to the monstrous
solicitations of her own father. In process of time Offa I.
married her. In Offa II. the story is altered and enlarged,
but it is manifestly the same legend of which we have
the earliest form in Beowulf.

Wolzogen, in a note to his translation of Beowulf,
thinks that Modthrytho (Mod*trud*) answers to the Ger-
trude of Shakespear's Hamlet, and that 'Heming's son'
is Hamlet himself.

Thruðr, the Norse form of Thrytho, was the name of
one of the Vælkyries. In German this word passed into
the provincial *trude* with the signification of witch. Hans
Sachs, Grimm says, uses *alte trute* in that sense frequently
(D. M. 394). In English the beautiful conception of
northern mythology has sunk even lower, for—'to such
base uses may we come'—it still exists perhaps in our
'old trot' disrespectfully applied to an old woman.

---

* "Anno Domini DCCLXXXVIII. Sanguis de cælo in terram
profluxit, et regina *Ricdritha* diem extremum clausit." (Matt.
Paris, Chron. Majora, vol. i. p. 352.)

Note Q.

OHTHERE'S SONS.

The story of Eanmund and Eadgils, and indeed the whole of the history contained in this part of the poem, is told in such a fragmentary way—partly in the narrative here—partly in Beowulf's speech—partly in the middle of the fight with the dragon—and partly in the political disquisitions of the messenger—that it would still seem very confused even if the names of the actors and the sequence of events were more familiar to us than they are. In reality, however, it is simpler than it looks.

For the parentage of the young man, see Genealogical Table II. in Note B.

It was probably to assert a right—real or supposed—to the Swedish throne after the death of Ongentheow that Eanmund and Eadgils rebelled against their uncle Onela and, failing in their attempt, took refuge with the young king of the Goths Heardred. Onela seems to have pursued them, and in the fighting that followed Eanmund was killed by Wohstan (l. 2612). Heardred was also killed at this time, either by accident or by treachery, for he was at banquet when he was slain (l. 2384–6). Beowulf now took the kingdom, and attacked Onela both in revenge and to help Eadgils (2392), and Onela was killed (2396).

The feud, however, between Swedes and Goths was of long standing, and the defeat and slaughter of Ongentheow (told at length in the messenger's speech, 2922–2998) was evidently Higelac's proudest achievement, for (1968) he is called the "destroyer of Ongentheow."

Beowulf, although by his father's side a member of the royal Swedish race, the Scylfings, seems to have cast his lot entirely with his mother's family, among whom he had been brought up; and one at least of his Scylfing kinsmen followed him, for although Wohstan fought under Onela in a hostile expedition against the Goths, his son Wiglaf was Beowulf's most faithful friend and succeeded him as the "last of their Wægmund race" (2813).

Heyne, surely most unnecessarily, reads *feónd* for *freónd* in l. 2394. The alteration seemed to me to make the story hopelessly unintelligible.

NOTE R.

"A death unpriced."

"The death of a relative even if accidental must be avenged or atoned for by a compensation. *Let him buy or bear the spear* is an Anglo-Saxon legal phrase; that is, let him endure or buy off the feud. Tacitus states this to have been the case in his time, and every line of Teutonic poetry demonstrates the continuance of the custom. All old Teutonic law rests upon it as a principle. Hrethel as the *mundbora* or legal guardian of his son was bound to exact satisfaction, and was only prevented from doing so by parental affection. Why the deed should be called *feohleás* I cannot understand; the difficulty of settling a family occurrence of this kind can hardly have been so very great, or the case so very rare, in the times whose manners and habits are represented in Beowulf. It seems very clear that Hæðcyn was not even compelled to leave the land, since we find him peaceably succeeding his father Hreðel on the throne." (Kemble's Beowulf, vol. ii. Appendix).

Note S.

"God's light he chose."

Kemble remarks on this use of *ceósan*, which contrasts curiously with *niman* (to take), as in *se þe hine deáð nimeð* (441), 'he whom death shall take;' *gif mec deáð nimeð* (447), 'if death shall take me;' *hine wyrd forman* (1205), 'Weird took him,' etc., "Perhaps it is the Christian formula opposed to the old heathen belief in the personal agency of Death, Hell, the Wælcyrian (choosers of the slain), etc.; conf. l. 5632 [Grein, 2818], *ǽr he bǽl cure, priusquam rogum elegerit.*" (Kemble's Beowulf, vol. ii. Appendix.)

A further trace of heathenism occurs perhaps in the phrases *gif mec hild nime* (1481), 'if battle taketh me;" *gúð fornam* (1123), 'war had taken;' and *gúð nimeð* (2536), 'let death take.' Grimm thinks Hild and Gúd here are two of the Wælkyries called in the Norse 'Hildr' (Gray's 'Hilda') and 'Gunnr' (= Guðr). D. M. 393.

Note T.

WIGLAF'S DENUNCIATION.

"It is not improbable that the whole of this denunciation of Wiglaf is a judicial formulary: such we know early existed and in regular rhythmical measure." (Kemble's Beowulf, vol. ii. App. The whole note is full of interesting matter, but it is too long for extract and can hardly be abridged.)

Note U.

THE PLUNDERING OF THE HOARD BY WIGLAF.

The plundering of a sepulchral mound or hidden treasure was esteemed a great feat among the Norsemen, chiefly, I suppose, by reason of the supernatural terrors the robber had to brave, and it is often numbered among the achievements of a hero ; or, in Scott's words—

> " Of chiefs who, guided through the gloom
> By the pale death lights of the tomb,
> Ransacked the graves of warriors old,
> Their falchions wrenched from corpses' hold,
> Waked the deaf tomb with war's alarms,
> And bade the dead arise to arms ! "
> *Lay of the Last Minstrel*, C. vi. xxii.

The Saga of Hördr the son of Grimkell contains a wild and very fine story of the performance of this feat. (Islendinga Sögur, vol. ii. p. 43.)

Something of the same spirit may be traced in the account of the plundering of the dragon's hoard by Wiglaf, and something of the deep-rooted superstition that a curse lay upon all such treasures, may be seen in the melancholy words of the poet about the uselessness to mankind of all the wealth won by Wiglaf's prowess, as well as in the rather obscure passage about the spell laid on it by its first possessor. At a later time this belief found utterance in the Eddic story of the Andvaranaut and the fate of the Niflungs, and yet more splendidly in the German version of the same tale. And so in the Saga of Hördr, Soti lays a curse on the ring that the hero takes from him when his last resting-place is broken into. A still later age said that fairy money turned into leaves or pebbles.

Riches, says Pope—

> "No grace of heaven or token of th' elect ;
> Giv'n to the fool, the mad, the vain, the evil,
> To Ward, to Waters, Chartres, and the *devil*."
>
> *Moral Essays*, Ep. iii.

NOTE V.

If the poem had not unluckily been in such a ruinous condition at this place we might perhaps have learned more of the ceremonies which attended the burning of a chieftain's body—a point on which very little seems to be known. One is tempted to believe that the 'elf-locked crone' here is the old woman who at the cremation of a Norse warrior bore a principal part in the ceremony, and was called 'the dead man's angel.' It was her duty to prepare the corpse, and to kill, or assist in killing, the poor creature—wife or handmaiden—who had agreed to be burned with her lord and accompany him to the other world. It would be rash to conjecture that any hint of this horrible custom is to be found in the few scattered syllables which are all that is left of the next four lines, but there can, I suppose, be little doubt that the ceremonial at burning was much the same among the Goths and Danes as among Norsemen. See, in the Proceedings of the Society of Antiquaries of Scotland for 1872, a very curious "Description by Ahmed Ibn Fozlan (an eye-witness) of the ceremonies attending the incremation of the dead body of a Norse chief, written in the early part of the tenth century, translated from Holmboe's Danish version of the Arabic original," by Mr. Joseph Anderson. An abstract of this paper is given in Burton's History of Scotland, 2nd edition, vol. i. p. 109, note. Ibn Fozlan was ambassador from the Khalif Muktedir to the king of the Bulgarians in 922.

PRINTED BY WILLIAM CLOWES AND SONS, LIMITED,
LONDON AND BECCLES.

Lightning Source UK Ltd.
Milton Keynes UK
UKHW020906230119
336059UK00010B/513/P